GEORGE M. PISKURICH
AND
ETHAN S. SANDERS

ASTD MODELS
FOR
LEARNING
TECHNOLOGIES

ROLES,
COMPETENCIES,
AND
OUTPUTS

ASTD

Ordering Information: Books published by the American Society for Training & Development can be ordered by calling 800.628.2783.

1640 King Street
Box 1443
Alexandria, VA 22313-2043
PH 703.683.8100, FX 703.683.8103
www.astd.org

Library of Congress Catalog Card Number: 98-070403

ISBN: 1-56286-083-6

TABLE OF CONTENTS

◢ LIST OF FIGURES AND TABLES

The recent influx of learning technologies into organizations has created quite a challenge for human resource development professionals. While these technologies hold great potential for our profession, they also create the need for new competencies. The 21st century has arrived, and HRD professionals need to find innovative ways of meeting new demands such as lower cost training, more accessible training, more meaningful learning experiences, just-in-time delivery of information, and more performance-centered instruction.

This volume, published by the American Society for Training & Development, serves as a handbook, guide, and tool for those involved in applying learning technologies within organizations. This is an important and seminal study that is likely to influence the future use of learning technologies for many years to come. It is intended to serve the ASTD community and all people who face the challenges that accompany the implementation of learning technologies.

ASTD Models for Learning Technologies directs attention to the roles, competencies, outputs, ethical issues, future forces, and other issues affecting those involved in implementing learning technologies. Although this study follows in the footsteps of other ASTD studies, it used new techniques for gathering data, classifying the technologies, and presenting the findings. It now joins the proud heritage of the ASTD competency series.

This study is among many products that ASTD offers in its continuing quest to provide the finest professional development opportunities to its members. Another proud accomplishment is ASTD's joint sponsorship of the Interactive Multimedia conferences on new learning technologies. Along with our cosponsor, the Society for Applied Learning Technology (SALT®), we hope to continue bringing the cutting-edge information that our members have come to expect. We are delighted to provide these resources and believe they will contribute greatly to the body of knowledge that is constantly transforming our profession.

I wish to acknowledge and express my appreciation to the principal authors, George Piskurich and Ethan Sanders, who also served as project manager, and to the contributing authors, Laurie J. Bassi, Scott Cheney, Greta Kotler, Ed Schroer, and Mark Van Buren. Also I am grateful for the many advisors who guided this project through its journey. There are simply too many to list here. One of the great strengths of this study is how people from all parts of this organization worked together towards a common goal. We are very proud of their achievement.

Curtis Plott

Curtis E. Plott
President and CEO
American Society for Training & Development

In the 1997 National HRD Executive Survey on Learning Technologies, conducted by ASTD's research department, human resource development managers indicated that keeping up with new technology is one of the top challenges they face today. Long before this study was conducted, however, there was clear evidence that technology would play an increasing role in the training profession. In the 1989 study *ASTD Models for HRD Practice*, two of the top 10 future forces for HRD work involved an increased reliance on sophisticated technology ("Increased sophistication and a variety of tools, technologies, methods, theories, and choices in HRD" and "Increased use of systems approaches that integrate HRD systems and technology in the workplace," p. 13, McLagan, 1989). These predictions have come to pass. Today ASTD continually receives requests from its members for more information on learning technologies. This increased demand has led ASTD to develop numerous studies, publications, and other products to help fill the information gap. These products and services include

◆ a 1997 Trends Update, published in the November 1997 issue of *Training & Development* magazine
◆ 14 *Info-line* publications, including "Basics of EPSS," "Basics of Internet Technology," "Improve Training with Interactive Multimedia," and so forth
◆ a 1998 Performance Improvement course, which focuses on learning technologies
◆ 16 presentations and one workshop on learning technologies at ASTD's 1997 International Conference and Exposition
◆ seven presentations and one workshop at the 1997 Technical Training Conference and Exposition
◆ a 20 percent increase in articles on learning technologies for *Training & Development* and *Technical Training* magazines in 1997 over the previous year
◆ joint sponsorship of the Interactive Multimedia conferences with the Society for Applied Learning Technology (SALT®)
◆ "Benchmarking Service Best Practices in Learning Technology" supplement in *Training & Development* magazine
◆ online forum on learning technologies
◆ learning technology Web site
◆ the learning technology series of books
◆ online learning seminar delivered via the teleconference series.

While all of this information represents an important start, it is essential to understand that much more information is needed on this subject. HRD professionals are frequently required to deploy training programs over existing distribution channels that have not been specifically designed for training purposes. HRD professionals require a technical understanding of the equipment they need to use and a clear understanding of the benefits that this new technology offers. Also HRD professionals need a clear understanding of where the HRD function fits into this new world of technology. All of these challenges create a great need for more information.

When supplying this information, it is essential to remember who the audience is. Many people who currently implement learning technologies do not come from an HRD background, nor do they report to the HR/HRD department. This new breed of trainer has emerged from front line managers and subject matter experts who have been given additional training responsibilities. In the 21st century organization, it is likely that the lines separating training, computing, and communication will continue to blur. New information on learning technologies must include practical methods for adding value to the organization in such an environment.

Although this study can't answer every question related to learning technologies, it is a critical piece in a much larger puzzle. Furthermore, learning technologies must always be viewed within the broader context of improving human performance. It is important that the cost effectiveness of learning technologies never be used as an excuse for reverting to the belief that training is always the best intervention for solving performance problems. Only after a detailed performance analysis has been performed—and training has been deemed the most appropriate intervention—can learning technologies even begin to be considered. Ultimately, the decision to use learning technologies must be based on the needs of the learners and the instructors.

◢ ACKNOWLEDGMENTS

Learning Technologies Expert Panel[1]

Nina Adams
President
Adams Consulting Group, Inc.
Western Springs, Illinois

Robert Barthelemy
Director
Universal Technology Corporation
Dayton, Ohio

Henry Berman
Principal
Solutions by Design
Needham, Massachusetts

Alan Chute
Chief Learning Strategist
Lucent Technologies: Center for Excellence in
Distance Learning
Cincinnati, Ohio

Larry Conley
Manager of Education and Training and
    FORDSTAR, Sales, Marketing and Service
Ford Motor Company
Dearborn, Michigan

Caitlin Curtin
President & CEO
Luminare
San Francisco, California

Bart Dahmer
Managing Director
Federal Express
Memphis, Tennessee

Lance Dublin
Chairman & CEO
Dublin Group
San Francisco, California

Paul Elliott
President
Human Performance Technologies
Annapolis, Maryland

Diane Gayeski
Partner
OmniCom Associates and Associate Professor of
    Corporate Communication
Ithaca College
Ithaca, New York

Brandon Hall
Editor
Multimedia & Internet Training Newsletter
Sunnyvale, California

Daryl Hunt
Senior Systems Engineer BTG
    Doctoral Candidate/Research Assistant
Pennsylvania State University
Bellefonte, Pennsylvania

Cissy Lennon
IVT Operation Manager
Federal Aviation Administration Academy
Oklahoma City, Oklahoma

Michael Marquardt
President
Global Learning Associates
Reston, Virginia

Elliott Masie
President
The Masie Center
Saratoga, New York

Inabeth Miller
Vice-President of Academic Affairs
Massachusetts Communications College
Boston, Massachusetts

George Piskurich
Principal
GMP Associates
Chapel Hill, North Carolina

Alexandra Rand
CEO
Internal & External Communication, Inc.
Marina Del Rey, California

Barry Raybould
President
Ariel Seminars
Pacific Grove, California

Angus Reynolds
Program Coordinator
Southern Illinois University
Albuquerque, New Mexico

Kim Ruyle
President & CEO
Plus Delta Performance, Inc.
La Crosse, Wisconsin

Harlan Seyfer
EDS China Training Manager
EDS China
Beijing, China

Neil Silverstein
Global Training Manager
Duracell International
Bethel, Connecticut

Barry Smith
Manager-Data General University
Data General Corporation
Westboro, Massachusetts

Advisory Panel

Phil Anderson, Sacha Cohen, Theresa Eversole,
Pat Galagan, Greta Kotler, Nancy Olson, Ed Schroer,
and Mark Van Buren.

---

[1] *The participation of the individuals listed above does not
constitute their agreement or disagreement with the results
of this study.*

◢ ABOUT THE AUTHORS

George M. Piskurich, Ph.D.

George Piskurich is an independent consultant based in the Raleigh/Durham area of North Carolina, where he provides consulting services and workshops in Instructional Design, Management Development, and Instructional Technology. His clients include *Fortune* 500 and *Fortune* 100 companies and run the gamut from high technology to banking to manufacturing. He can be contacted at 919.968.0878 or e-mail GMP1@Compuserve.com.

Ethan S. Sanders

Ethan Sanders is currently a project manager for ASTD in the Market Development Department. Before joining ASTD, he was a senior instructional designer of management development courses in the banking industry. He also coauthored the ASTD course "Human Performance Improvement in the Workplace." He holds a master's degree in applied behavior science from the Johns Hopkins University. He can be contacted at 703.683.9595 or e-mail esanders@astd.org.

◢ INTRODUCTION

"Learning technologies" is one of those concepts that defies description. Ask 25 practitioners to define it, and you would receive many different answers. In fact, we began our study by conducting several focus groups at the 1997 ASTD International Conference and Exposition in Washington, D.C. One of the questions that we asked the participants was, "What are learning technologies?" The first respondent said, "Virtual reality." After probing for a few moments, we discovered that she meant a simulated workplace that is identical to what the employee will experience on the job. We were also amazed to discover that she didn't necessarily believe this "virtual workplace" had to be simulated electronically. The second respondent, a gentleman from Germany, held up a ballpoint pen and claimed, "This too is a learning technology." This story illustrates how challenging it was to begin placing boundaries around this subject. The body of knowledge that the term "learning technologies" relates to is a moving target. Thirty years ago the most advanced learning technology was a broadcast-quality videotape; 20 years ago it was a branched, text-based CBT program; five years ago it was multimedia with digital video on a CD-ROM; today it is Web-based applications. In the next few years, we anticipate more realistic training simulations using three-dimensional modeling and virtual reality. Trying to guess what the most advanced technologies will be more than five years from now would require nearly clairvoyant competencies.

Looking back, we see the roots of learning technologies coupled with the emergence of the instructional systems design. Both reached maturity in the 1950s and 1960s when corporate, government, and military training departments began implementing the ISD process for systematically solving skill deficiencies, using 16 mm films and transparency projectors to assist instructors in delivering content. As ISD became more commonplace in training facilities, so did the use of records, filmstrips, audiotapes, slides, videos, and, eventually, the computer. While ISD has remained fairly constant over the past four decades, the types of technologies and the amount of their usage has begun to change. More importantly, the rate of change among these technologies is expected to accelerate exponentially over the next five years. Even though these technologies are subject to change, some form of definition and delineation is nevertheless critical for our profession.

In professions such as engineering or health care, the tools and techniques that practitioners employ have changed drastically over the past 100 years. In training, however, the time-honored tradition of one human being teaching another has only begun to change in recent years. Even considering the aforementioned growth of classroom technologies such as the transparency projector and videos, instructors still deliver the overwhelming majority of content in a classroom. The 1997 National HRD Executive Survey on Learning Technologies asked training managers how much of their training is being delivered via technology currently and how much will be delivered via technology in the future (see Appendix B for more details). For 1996, respondents reported that 80 percent of their training was instructor led, 10 percent was delivered via learning technologies, and 10 percent was delivered via other methods. For 1997, these same respondents estimated that 72 percent of their training would be instructor led, 17 percent would be delivered via learning technologies, and 11 percent would be delivered via other methods. When asked to forecast their delivery methods for the year 2000, they predicted that 55 percent of their training would be instructor led, 35 percent would be delivered via learning technologies, and 10 percent via other means. This is an extraordinary shift toward relying on technology to deliver content (see figure 1).

This shift leaves our profession in a challenging position. Organizations are clamoring for less expensive, more accessible, and more effective training. Although limited research has been conducted on learning retention rates using technologies, the evidence is pouring in that learning technologies are cheaper and more accessible than traditional classroom instruction. This evidence alone will propel organizations towards relying more on learning technologies for educating their employees. Human resource development professionals need to recognize the tremendous potential that these technologies bring to the field of adult education. They must also continue to play a role in deciding how and when to use these technologies. Without a coherent and generally accepted description of these technologies, it is difficult to play a role in this process, let alone to discuss it with our colleagues, external clients, and internal clients.

This project is best seen as an exploration. ASTD sought to get a general idea of what it takes for HRD professionals to select and manage these technologies and what their likely role is in the implementation and support of these technologies. To collect data on this topic, we carefully selected leading experts in the field to give us their perspective of what competencies are needed to select, manage, and use these technologies. The classification system and definitions contained within this exploration will help to clear away some of the ambiguity surrounding learning technologies and help establish a common language for this topic.

Even the term "learning technology" can be confusing. During the literature search, many terms were discovered that essentially describe the same idea. These terms include instructional technology, technology-based training, technology-based learning, technology-assisted learning, technology-mediated instruction, and a host of other possibilities. Although some of these terms may be grammatically more accurate, or are more commonplace in some organizations, learning technologies seems to be the term that most HRD professionals recognize when describing the technologies that are used for developing skills and knowledge.

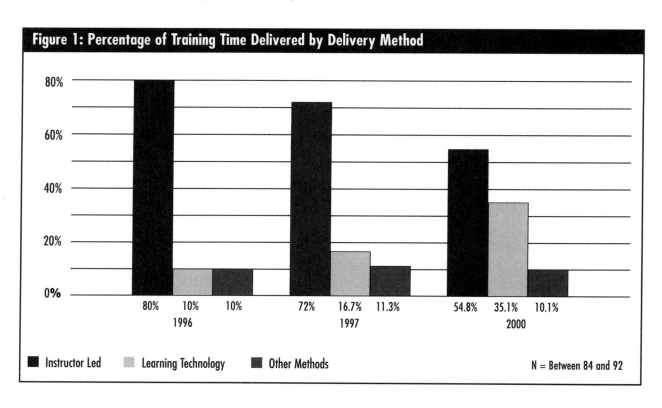

Figure 1: Percentage of Training Time Delivered by Delivery Method

80%

60%

40%

20%

0%

| 80% | 10% | 10% | | 72% | 16.7% | 11.3% | | 54.8% | 35.1% | 10.1% |
| 1996 | | | | 1997 | | | | 2000 | | |

■ Instructor Led   ▨ Learning Technology   ■ Other Methods   N = Between 84 and 92

SECTION 1 DESCRIPTION OF THE STUDY
By Ethan S. Sanders

Deciding What to Study

As mentioned previously, ASTD began its exploration of learning technologies by asking groups of practitioners to define specific technologies as well as learning technologies as a whole. It was a challenge to reach a consensus during these focus groups. In particular, participants found that it was difficult to define the technologies because they believed that the definition would change based on how the technology was being used. For instance, the definition of a CD-ROM is quite different depending on if it is carrying audio, video, text, or a combination of the three. Opinions also varied on whether the word "technology" necessarily means electronic technologies, whether there needs to be a distinction between formal "learning" and informal "information," and whether performance support systems are actually learning technologies.

Deciding How to Study Learning Technologies

The need to establish boundaries around this topic soon became apparent. Based on a large number of responses from the focus groups, ASTD decided to center the research on electronic technologies that deliver content to the learner and not what might be called "support" technologies such as authoring tools, course registration software, or design assistance tools. While these support technologies play an integral role in delivering training, they do not have the express purpose of enhancing the development of skills and knowledge.

ASTD modeled this on past competency studies, specifically, the 1989 *ASTD Models for HRD Practice* (McLagan) and the 1996 *ASTD Models for Human Performance Improvement* (Rothwell). Using the competency-based approach was advantageous because it permitted the study to

◆ focus on the practitioner's role in applying learning technologies rather than focus on the technologies themselves
◆ avoid becoming outdated as soon as the technologies change
◆ allow the respondents to frame their responses in familiar terms
◆ allow the researchers to consider roles and competencies that existed in this profession before the introduction of technology and determine which ones are still relevant in the process of selecting, managing, and using learning technologies.

This competency approach created a document that is useful to practitioners and reflects the current desire of HRD professionals to understand their emerging roles in the world of technology. After establishing the scope of this study, ASTD followed a competency research methodology using these steps:

1. Form an internal advisory committee.
2. Create a theoretical framework.
3. Conduct an extensive literature review.
4. Select an expert panel.
5. Create survey instruments.
6. Collect and analyze data.
7. Refine competency and output lists.
8. Write and revise a report.

◆ **Internal advisory committee:** Representatives from many ASTD departments served on the internal advisory committee. The panel consisted of staff members from departments such as Publications, Market Development, New Business Development, Strategic Planning Department, and Research. The primary responsibilities of the committee were to select members for the external expert panel, create a project framework, refine the lists of competencies and outputs that were generated from the literature review, and critique the final manuscript.
◆ **Theoretical framework:** Before embarking on the project's research phase, it was essential to nail down the theoretical underpinnings of this subject. Enclosed as Section 3 is the entire framework that was used for thinking about learning technologies. Researchers updated the framework continuously and gave all expert panel members the opportunity to review the framework and submit any changes.
◆ **Literature review:** The literature review covered over 250 articles from 38 magazines, journals, and books that were published from 1994 to the present. The initial database search of articles included titles such as learning technology, Internet training, multimedia instruction, computer-based training (CBT), technology-assisted learning, distance education, and all the permutations and combinations of these terms. Most of the articles described the use, selection, and management of the technologies themselves and gave important "how to" tips. The literature reviewers needed to infer what skills and knowledge would enable an HRD professional to follow this advice. They then searched for patterns within these descriptions and

grouped like skills and knowledge under more generic competency descriptions. In addition to analyzing the books and articles, the literature reviewers carefully considered all of the competency descriptions from the previous two ASTD competency studies. Those that applied to the use and management of learning technologies were included in this study. The final product of this review was a comprehensive list of 31 competencies and 45 outputs related to learning technologies.

◆ **Expert panel:** The expert panel for this project represented the numerous specialties within the field of learning technologies. All panel members met the following criteria and specialized in areas such as multimedia development, electronic performance support systems (EPSS), broadcast TV, CBT, virtual reality, and groupware. The selection criteria used to choose the expert panel members were

1. demonstrated commitment and contribution to the field of HRD and reputation for specialty in learning technologies

Considerations:
◆ major projects the nominee has developed and the objectives and outcomes of each
◆ theories the nominee has developed and information on how they have been used
◆ articles, books, videos, and programs that the nominee has published and critiques of those publications

2. evidence of influence upon other HRD professionals

Considerations:
◆ participation and contribution to professional societies
◆ use of those societies' theories and practices

3. evidence of national or international acclaim for work within the HRD field

Considerations:
◆ awards and honorary degrees
◆ major speaking engagements
◆ appearances in films, videos, or TV programs to share the nominee's theories.

This expert panel never met in person. Instead, all communication was conducted via Internet e-mail, electronic survey software, fax, and phone. Researchers first contacted the experts by phone to determine their interest in participating in the study. If their answer was affirmative, they were sent the study's framework and asked to critique it by answering the following questions:
1. Does this framework represent a logical assessment of the relationship among HRD roles, instructional systems design (ISD), and learning technologies?
2. Do the classifications and definitions match your understanding of how learning technologies are currently being used in the profession?
3. What instructional methods, presentation methods, or distribution methods were missed?
4. Are there other specific areas that need to be added?
5. How useful will this study be for you when it is completed?
6. What issues regarding competencies for learning technologies would you like future studies to address?

When the lists of competencies were ready, researchers sent the expert panel members an electronic questionnaire through e-mail. Finally, expert panel members were given the opportunity to write a short article on "The Future of Learning Technologies" (see Appendix A).

◆ **Survey instruments:** After the list of competencies had been refined, researchers created a questionnaire that allowed respondents to assess the accuracy of the competency's description, rate the importance of the competency to the field, and state which of the eight roles the competency applied to. Figure 1.1 shows the layout of the questionnaire and the wording of a typical question.

Figure 1.1: Example of First Questionnaire

Learning Technologies Competencies Survey

Below you will find 48 competency titles and descriptions. For each one please answer these four questions: a) Is the competency described accurately? b) Which role(s) does this competency apply to? (see project framework for role descriptions) c) How important is this competency for the use and management of learning technologies? d) Do you have any additional comments about the competency? Each competency will be numbered, and the above questions will have their corresponding letter next to the competency number (for example, 1a, 1b, 1c, 1d)

1. Adult Learning: Understanding how adults learn and how they use knowledge, skills, and attitudes.

1a. Is the competency described accurately? (If no, please explain why in the comment box.)

[**x**] Yes   [ ] No   [ ] Unsure

1b. Which role(s) does this competency apply to? Rank your answers, beginning with "7" as the most applicable role for this competency. If the competency doesn't apply to the role, leave that answer blank.

[4] HRD Manager

[6] Change Agent

[3] Analyst

[7] Designer

[5] Developer

[2] Implementor

[1] Evaluator

1c) How important is this competency to the overall use and management of learning technologies?
[**x**] Very important
[ ] Important
[ ] Somewhat Important
[ ] Unimportant

1d) Comments:

The experts were also asked to write in any competencies and roles that they thought were missing. Researchers compiled these write-ins and sent them back to all the experts for the same analysis. Because the expert feedback suggested drastic reorganization and many new descriptions of the competencies, a third questionnaire became necessary to reassess which roles applied to which competencies. Figure 1.2 shows the third questionnaire.

Figure 1.2: Example of Third Questionnaire

Competency Name and Description

For each role, rank the competency as either
- **0** does not apply,
- **1** somewhat important,
- **2** important,
- **3** very important

Sample:

1) Adult Learning: Understanding how adults learn and how they use knowledge, skills, and attitudes.

HRD Manager	Analyst	Designer	Developer	Change Agent	Implementor	Instructor	Evaluator
3	3	2	1	2	2	3	1

SECTION 2   FUTURE FORCES
By George M. Piskurich

It is important to consider all of the internal and external forces that influence organizational performance in order to understand fully the benefits of learning technologies. Here are some of the organizational forces that might affect the use of technology in the future, as well as some emerging technologies:

◆ **Skills training** will continue to be a major focus for companies as new jobs are created and current jobs change dramatically. Technology has been, and will continue to be, a dominant factor in the delivery of this aspect of employee development.

◆ **Computer skills training** is a subset of skills training, but needs to be discussed here in its own right. It is constantly in the top five responses to HRD trend polls, and more and more companies are beginning to realize that the way to teach computer skills is with the computer. Technology-based programs that use proper adult learning methodologies will reinforce classroom processes and reduce classroom time for the learning of these basic skills.

◆ **Continued corporate restructuring** and the cost-reduction requirements it engenders will increase the pressure for more efficient training. Technology used in the appropriate situations will continue to provide measurable, often significant, reductions in both direct and indirect training costs.

◆ **Downsizing of HRD departments** will require that more be done with less. Application of proper technology will help to meet this challenge by using corporate knowledge resources more effectively and by helping current HRD staffs to multiply their effectiveness by allowing them to be in more than one place at the same time.

◆ **The focus on performance** in many corporations will require the development of new performance-improvement tools. Because of modern business operations' complexity and reliance on technology, many of these tools will need to be technology based.

◆ **The transformation of companies into learning organizations** will require new technology-based infrastructures that facilitate the sharing of corporate knowledge and the achievement and evaluation of integrated goals.

◆ **The need to use the best possible resources** will further the emphasis on hiring disabled and minority employees. Technology will help to make these employees effective and efficient contributors to the organization.

◆ **Changing work habit patterns** will require organizations to create alternative work processes for their employees. Many of these processes, such as telecommuting and virtual offices, are technology-based interventions.

◆ **Accountability** will continue to be a major issue at all levels of the organization. Technology helps provide the necessary structure to determine accountability.

Concurrent with these organizational forces are evolving views concerning learning psychology that will affect the use of technology in the future:

◆ **Learner control** is an issue that has been gaining in emphasis for a number of years. Technology will provide increasing learner control, not only over when things are learned, but also how they are learned and even what is important to be learned for specific jobs and situations.

◆ **Individual responsibility for personal development** has become the new philosophy of development specialists. This vast need for programs and opportunities that can be employed on an individual basis will be met through the use of technology development, implementation, and administrative systems.

◆ **Self-directed learning theory** will challenge and assist those who work with technology to develop an integrated implementation format that will combine the suitable amount of technology and nontechnology-based learning interventions to meet the needs of learners who have lower and higher levels of internal self-directedness.

And last, but certainly not least, are the technologies that will be future forces in their own right:

◆ **Web-based training** through both internal and external Nets will continue to develop and become a standard for technology-based training as problems with bandwidth and speed are solved.

◆ **Desktop training and conferencing** will continue to grow as more employees become comfortable with on-demand learning at their fingertips and meetings that don't require them to leave the office, let alone the city, to attend.

◆ **Interactive distance learning**, either through satellite or land-line linkages, will become the preferred method of training for multinational corporations that can't afford the expense or, more importantly, the time to bring contributors to a central location for training.

- **High-definition television** will create a rebirth in the use of video for both live and prerecorded training programs.
- **Portable computers** that can be conveniently carried will provide EPSS and just-in-time training in any environment, from a factory floor to the inside of a military battle tank.
- **Voice recognition** will allow for data input without the use of cumbersome keyboards and mice. This will create a revolution in the development of expert systems as it will be possible to ask for the help of technology in the same way that people can ask for help of each other.

- **Personal communications devices** will provide wireless real-time access to information, and thus provide up-to-date training anywhere, anytime.
- **Virtual reality** processes will provide true simulations that will allow trainees to experience real situations without the real dangers. From three-dimensional models to total immersion, this technology will take training from theory to practice in a totally controlled environment.

For a more detailed analysis of future forces, Appendix C is a complete reprint of the article "Training Industry Trends 1997," which was published in the November 1997 issue of *Training & Development* magazine.

Purpose

The purpose of this framework is to state the fundamentals of this topic. This framework also outlines the boundaries of the study and can be thought of as a strawman that defines the competency study on learning technologies and the value it will have for the HRD community.

The ASTD Competency Program Series

ASTD has a continuing program for updating its analysis of the roles and competencies of HRD professionals. Its last comprehensive study was done in 1989. A more focused study on the emerging roles associated with human performance improvement was published in 1996. A continuing scan of customer requirements shows an urgent need for another study, this time on competencies for learning technologies. A close reading of the previous two competency studies shows that although they did not focus on learning technologies, they did anticipate their increased use.

Trends in HRD

The ASTD competency studies all try to anticipate trends. This study builds on the trends published in the November 1997 issue of *Training & Development* magazine (see Appendix C).

Relationship Between Human Performance Improvement and Learning Technologies

It is important to understand the role that learning technologies play in the broader context of human performance improvement. As defined here, learning technologies are being used for delivering information and for developing skills and knowledge (that is, instructional activities) and not for other types of management interventions. A proper performance analysis must precede the decision to use training activities as the correct intervention. It is assumed that training has already been determined to be the appropriate intervention before deciding whether using learning technologies is appropriate.

Scope of the Study

For purposes of this study, electronic technologies such as computer-mediated learning, satellite TV learning, and videotape are being examined. While certain nonelectronic technologies can be used to deliver training to a dispersed population (job aids, workbooks, mentoring, and so forth), ASTD's members are clearly seeking advice on how to best implement electronic technologies in their workplaces.

Learning technologies, as used here, refers to electronic technologies that deliver information and facilitate the development of skills and knowledge. Not included are support technologies that are used for course design, production, and management. The majority of these support technologies are software applications that assist with word processing, multimedia authoring, database management, performance management, logistics management, course registration, and so forth. Although these support technologies play an integral role in course design and management, they are not the actual technologies that deliver learning to trainees. The ability to use these technologies is assumed in the various roles, outputs, and competencies that are listed in this study.

A Classification System for Learning Technologies

One of the tools that has been sorely lacking in the study of learning technologies is a classification system that organizes these complex and diverse applications. The following classification system divides learning technologies into two major categories: presentation methods (see table 3.2) and distribution methods (see table 3.3). The third component of delivering information via technology is the instructional method. An instructional method represents how the information is taught to the learners. Instructional methods existed long before the advent of learning technologies and include such activities as lecture, role plays, games, and case studies (see table 3.1). Instructional methods are distinct from presentation methods and distribution methods because they do not depend on technology. For example, a lecture or role play can easily be delivered live and in person. At the same time, when training is delivered via technology, instructional methods are interwoven with presentation and distribution methods. When this occurs, all three methods combine to form a delivery process.

Perhaps the distinction between presentation methods and distribution methods can be best understood using the analogy of getting a message to another person. Depending on the message, the presentation methods may take a number of different formats: a letter, a package, an e-mail note, a telegram, or a phone call. For each presentation method, there exists one or more methods of actually transmitting the message. These distribution methods could include air mail, mail by sea, express delivery, facsimile machine, or telegraph. Certain presentation methods may only be transmitted via one distribution method (for example, telegram via telegraph), while others can have an array of distribution options (for example, a letter distributed via fax, air mail, express mail, and so forth). Regardless of which method is chosen, the decision ultimately pairs a presentation method with a distribution method. The key question underlying this distinction, therefore, is, "Is this technology a means of transmitting material or the format of the material itself?" This classification system is important for several reasons:

- **It shows the range of choices available.** It is very useful for practitioners to consider their full range of options when considering which presentation and distribution method to pair together.
- **It displays the interrelationship between the technologies.** It is difficult to plan, design, or deliver content via learning technologies without understanding how a presentation method can be delivered via several distribution methods or how a distribution method can handle several presentation methods. For instance, a CD-ROM can be used to deliver multimedia, full-motion video, or electronic text. Likewise, multimedia presentations can be delivered via CD-ROM, Intranet, or Internet. See table 3.4 for the full display of the interrelationships.
- **It links selecting and implementing learning technologies to the ISD model.** The stages of the ISD model have a direct relationship to the use of learning technologies. In general, the roles of designer, developer, and implementor are most affected by the introduction of learning technologies (see figure 3.1 on page 11 for more detail).
- **It allows better definition of the individual technologies.** It is impossible to create accurate definitions within this subject without understanding the potential roles each method can play in the delivery process.
- **It highlights the complex set of decision criteria that a person must consider.** This selection process is a balancing act between the best way to engage the learner (instructional method combined with presentation method) versus the limitations of the company's technological infrastructure (distribution methods). For example, a simulation via multimedia might be the best way to replicate a work environment, but if half the training population only has access to "dumb terminals," multimedia is probably not a viable option.
- **It creates a common point of reference for the profession.** This model will create a foundation for building future discussions.

Table 3.1: Instructional Methods

Case Study
Demonstration
Expert Panels
Games
Group Discussion
Lecture
Practical Exercise
Programmed Instruction
Reading
Role Play
Simulation

Table 3.2: Presentation Methods

Audio
CBT
Electronic Text
EPSS
Groupware
Interactive TV
Multimedia
Online Help
Teleconferencing
3D Modeling/Virtual Reality
Video

Table 3.3: Distribution Methods

Audiotape
Cable TV
CD-ROM
Computer Disk
Digital Video Disk (DVD)
Electronic Mail
Extranet
Internet
Intranet
LAN/WAN
Satellite TV
Tactile Gear/Simulator
Telephone
Videotape
Voice Mail
World Wide Web

Although any system of classification has its exceptions, this classification system helps to identify the commonalities among the technologies. In no way should the distinction between presentation methods and distribution methods imply that these technologies are independent of each other. These distinctions were made for the purpose of studying the similarities and differences between the technologies. In actual use these technologies are fully dependent on each other. This is the same approach a biologist would take when dissecting an organism, classifying the organs according to function (for example, neurological system, cardiovascular system, digestive system, and so forth), but never losing sight of the fact that none of the systems within the organism can function independently of each other.

The fact that new technologies will emerge that challenge this classification system does not nullify the value of classifying the technologies. Again, in biology all living organisms are classified according to a taxonomy (kingdom, phylum, class, order, family, genus, species). When the Swedish botanist Linnaeus (1707–1778) created his taxonomy, no one could have forecast the discovery of the duck-billed platypus in the late 1790s. Imagine the controversy among biologists when they discovered this beast that has a beak like a duck, a tail like a beaver, produces milk for its young, and lays eggs! Yet this discovery did not nullify the entire taxonomy of living things. Instead scientists had to reexamine their classification system and look for a new set of distinctions between birds and mammals. Today the duck-billed platypus resides comfortably in the taxonomy of living things as a monotreme. The point here is that radically new technologies will require reexamination and adjustment of this classification system, which is a worthwhile pursuit.

As table 3.4 shows, there are currently 11 distinguishable electronic presentation methods. This list

Table 3.4: Presentation Methods for Distribution Methods Abbreviated Matrix

Presentation Methods	Distribution Methods
Audio	LAN/WAN, Web, Intranet, Internet, Extranet, CD-ROM/DVD, Voice Mail, Audiotape, Telephone, Computer Disk
CBT	LAN/WAN, Web, Intranet, Internet, Extranet, CD-ROM/DVD, Computer Disk
Electronic Text	LAN/WAN, Web, Intranet, Internet, Extranet, CD-ROM/DVD, E-mail, Computer Disk
EPSS	LAN/WAN, Web, Intranet, Internet, Extranet, CD-ROM/DVD, Computer Disk
Groupware	LAN/WAN, Web, Intranet, Internet, Extranet, Computer Disk
Interactive TV	Satellite TV, Cable TV
Multimedia	LAN/WAN, Web, Intranet, Internet, Extranet, CD-ROM/DVD, Tactile Gear/Simulator, Computer Disk
Online Help	LAN/WAN, Web, Intranet, Internet, Extranet, CD-ROM/DVD, Computer Disk
Teleconferencing	Satellite TV, Cable TV, LAN/WAN, Internet, Intranet, Extranet, Telephone
3D Modeling/ Virtual Reality	CD-ROM/DVD, Tactile Gear/Simulator
Video	Satellite TV, Cable TV, LAN/WAN, Web, Intranet, Internet, Extranet, CD-ROM/DVD, Videotape, Computer Disk

will change and grow, but by studying the technologies that exist today, it will be easier to understand new ones as they come along. It is also important to appreciate the numerous ways that these technologies are being combined in the field. In general, however, the presentation methods and distribution methods fall into natural "clusters" of combined use (see table 3.4 or Appendix D for more detail).

Technologies are not simply one piece of equipment, but are systems that embody multiple hardware components and are often supported by software. There are, of course, numerous components that make up the technologies, including PC projectors, microphones, response systems, uplinks/downlinks, video cameras, interactions tablets, modems, servers, printers, tape players, and so forth. Although these are essential components, they are not used alone for the express purpose of "delivering information and facilitating the development of skills and knowledge." Therefore, they cannot be classified as learning technologies.

Many technologies have more than one popular name. For example, distance learning via satellite broadcasting is typically called "interactive television," but it is also described as "satellite systems," "business television," and "video teletraining." The term "distance learning" doesn't show up in the list of available technologies. The meaning of this term is ambiguous. In its broadest sense, distance learning denotes the separation of the source of information (the instructor) from the learner either geographically (different places) or temporally (different times). This definition of distance learning embraces a very large range of systems. In its popular use, however, distance learning usually refers to satellite-based interactive television. For these reasons distance learning should neither be used to refer to learning technologies in general, nor to describe interactive television specifically.

The Relationship Between ISD and Learning Technology

The instructional systems design model (ISD involves analysis, design, development, delivery, and evaluation) can be equated to the process of selecting and using learning technologies. The design, development, and delivery phases of the ISD model are the major areas affected by the introduction of learning technologies. These phases will involve expanded roles, increased competencies, and new outputs for practitioners. In general, the introduction of learning technologies does not dramatically affect the analysis and evaluation phases. The analysis phase still entails determining business needs, performance needs, and gaps in current performance. Evaluation continues to assess whether the learning objectives have been met; however, evaluation must be expanded to address the effectiveness of the technology used. Figure 3.1 outlines the key activities in each phase of the ISD process as it relates to learning technologies.

Types of Information About Technology

Whether planning a technologies mix for an entire company, choosing a particular mix for a course, or planning the design and development of course materials, there are certain basic considerations that have to be taken into account. These considerations require detailed comparisons of the needs of the learners, the needs of the organization, and the existing capabilities of the technological infrastructure of the company. Seven important categories of information must be considered during this analysis. The following questions help examine each category:

◆ **Components:** What hardware, software, and human elements make up the technology? How do they interact? What are their basic characteristics?
◆ **Needs:** How well does the technology address the adult learning needs of the trainee population? What are the demographics of the trainee population? What is the availability of the trainees (for example, are they all available at one time and in one place)? What are the organization's needs (for example, urgency of learning requirement, number of trainees per session, and so forth)?
◆ **Costs:** What are the acquisition costs, operational costs, and design costs associated with the technology?
◆ **Design:** How do you design and develop materials using this technology? Are there computerized design aids (for example, Designer's Edge) available to assist with this process?
◆ **Instruction:** How is the instruction being delivered (that is, live interactive learning or self-managed learning)?
◆ **Evaluation:** How will course objectives and technology effectiveness be measured for success?
◆ **Logistics:** What logistical arrangements are necessary for each learning technology?

Figure 3.1: Steps in ISD and Learning Technology Implementation Process

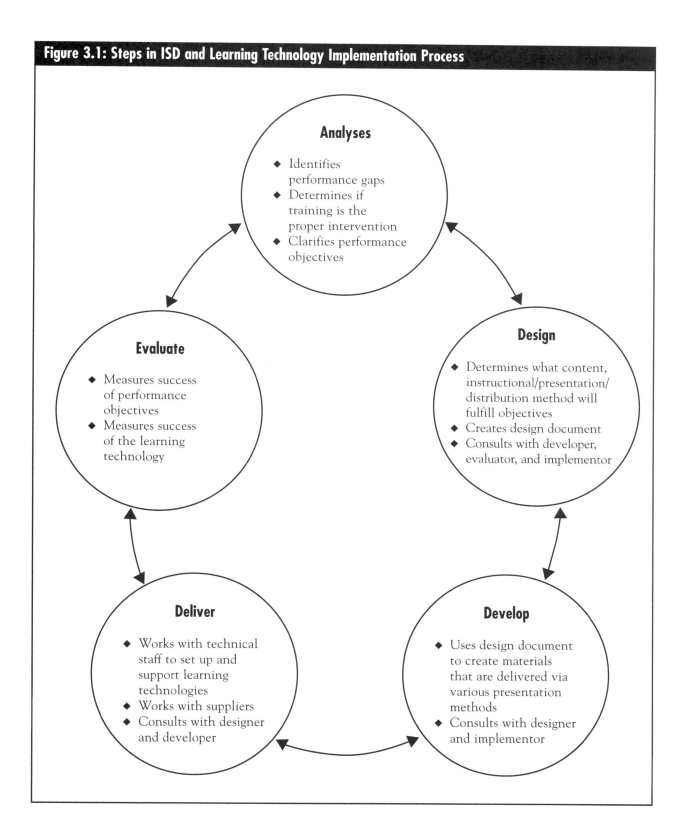

Analyses

- ◆ Identifies performance gaps
- ◆ Determines if training is the proper intervention
- ◆ Clarifies performance objectives

Design

- ◆ Determines what content, instructional/presentation/ distribution method will fulfill objectives
- ◆ Creates design document
- ◆ Consults with developer, evaluator, and implementor

Evaluate

- ◆ Measures success of performance objectives
- ◆ Measures success of the learning technology

Deliver

- ◆ Works with technical staff to set up and support learning technologies
- ◆ Works with suppliers
- ◆ Consults with designer and developer

Develop

- ◆ Uses design document to create materials that are delivered via various presentation methods
- ◆ Consults with designer and implementor

Outputs and Quality Requirements for Learning Technologies

ASTD Models for HRD Practice defined an output as "a product or service that an individual or group delivers to others, especially to colleagues, customers, or clients" and quality requirements as "the characteristics of a quality output" (McLagan, 1989, p. 77). McLagan also explained that the overriding question in the researcher's mind when developing lists of quality requirements is, "What must be true of this output in order for its users and HRD professionals to approve it?" In 1996, William Rothwell asserted that quality requirements need to be tied to more than just outputs (Rothwell, 1996, p. 30). He believes that in human performance improvement work, quality requirements can be tied to

◆ applications of the human performance improvement process model
◆ demonstrations of single or multiple roles
◆ demonstrations of competencies
◆ outputs.

Furthermore, Rothwell made a distinction between a "terminal output" ("a final outcome directly associated with a particular role") and an "enabling output" ("a specific output associated with the demonstration of a particular competency") (p. 79). This distinction helped to bridge the gap among quality requirements for outputs, quality requirements for roles, and quality requirements for competencies. It is challenging to determine what types of information will be the most useful to the average person who will use this book. As Rothwell points out in *ASTD Models for Human Performance Improvement*,

> [U]sers of *Models for HRD Practice* have often asked for measurable quality requirements, not just the criteria for measuring quality in HRD work, which are provided in that publication. Such a request assumes, with some naiveté, that all organizations and all decision makers possess identical expectations. Unfortunately, that is not always the case. Expectations for performance vary among organizations and among stakeholders and decision makers…Quality exists in the mind of the beholder—and the beholders may vary.

The decision to include quality requirements in this study was a far more pragmatic decision. During the literature search researchers compiled an enormous list of citations. These citations described the results that HRD professionals who are involved with learning technologies are expected to produce. As the list was organized it became apparent that there were two very different types of descriptions. Some of the descriptions were clearly deliverables (for example, "Training programs that teach technical skills"), while others were more akin to qualitative judgments (for example, "Training programs that are cost-effective and valuable to the client"). Faced with a decision of either discarding all of the citations that weren't tangible output descriptions or sorting the list into output descriptions and quality requirements of those outputs, the researchers decided to include the quality descriptions. These quality requirements may not be useful to all readers, but it is important that readers make their own determination as to whether this additional data is useful. This does not mean that Rothwell's assertion has been disregarded. The quality requirements provided in this study are just a guideline of some aspects to consider. They represent a partial list, and each quality requirement applies only in certain circumstance. Table 4.1 shows the relationship between outputs and quality requirements.

Competencies for Learning Technologies

A competency, as defined by McLagan, is "an area of knowledge or skill that is critical for producing key outputs" (McLagan, 1989, p. 77). As McLagan also points out, outputs describe the work of HRD professionals by answering the question "What do HRD practitioners provide?" Competencies, on the other hand, answer the question, "What knowledge and skills will enable people to do HRD work?" (McLagan, p. 43). The list of 31 competencies in table 4.2 on page 19 uses this same rationale, but adds a more specified question: "What knowledge and skills will enable people to select, manage, and use learning technologies for HRD work?"

The competencies have also been grouped into generic categories (general competencies, management competencies, distribution method competencies, and presentation method competencies), which helps to show the relationship among certain competencies. While these categories are helpful, they are not detailed enough to show how these competencies apply to the work of training professionals. Later in this section, tables 4.4 and 4.5 show which roles and outputs these competencies apply to. Core competencies, noted with an asterisk in table 4.2, were considered "important" or "very important" to at least five of the eight roles.

Table 4.1: Learning Technology Outputs and Quality Requirements

Outputs	Quality Requirements
1. Classroom environments	**Classroom environments that** • are conducive to effective learning • are equipped with advanced technologies • are monitored and updated continuously.
2. Communication systems	**Communication systems that** • connect learners, instructors, and subject matter experts together • are reliable • are easy to use.
3. Contracts for vendors to provide service 4. Contracts or agreements with management, clients (written or oral)	**Contracts that** • achieve agreement on desired results • contain clear logistics and schedules • contain clear terms and conditions • demonstrate commitment from all parties • are consistent with the organization's mission • are legally binding • develop long-term relationships • demonstrate a win-win negotiation process • produce realistic promises.
5. Equipment for learning	**Equipment that** • functions properly for the learner and the instructor • allows the learner to focus on the content • does not require a steep learning curve for use • is properly monitored and maintained.
6. Evaluation instruments	**Evaluation instruments that** • are accompanied by a clear set of instructions • ask relevant questions • are clearly written and easy to use • yield meaningful data • have been pilot tested • reflect practical constraints on administration • use appropriate instrumentation designs • are valid and reliable.
7. Guidelines for designers and developers 8. Guidelines for instructors and facilitators	**Guidelines that** • define performance requirements • account for short- and long-term needs • are accurate and complete • are adaptable • adhere to sound adult learning principles • are aligned with management priorities • are based on valid practices and methodologies • challenge people to rise to a higher level of performance • are clear and understandable • consider budgetary restrictions and requirements • contain realistic time frames • establish measurable goals and milestones • are ethically justifiable • are linked to observable behaviors

Outputs	Quality Requirements
9. Guidelines for needs analysts and evaluators	• meet learner and instructor needs • are periodically reviewed • are practical for decision making • reflect an understanding of the organization's culture and values • are relevant to organizational goals and objectives • take into account current forces, future forces, and trends.
10. Materials for the student (electronic and paper-based)	**Materials that** • are accurate and complete • can be easily revised • clearly communicate information or concepts • complement the design objectives • enhance the learning process • give additional references for continued learning • are grammatically accurate • are interactive • maintain the learner's interest • have been maintained and updated • meet the learner's needs • provide good value for the organization • provide a summary for the learner • are relevant to the course content • respect copyrights and trademarks • are user friendly.
11. Plans for choosing effective and efficient technology 12. Plans for converting classroom instructors into distance learning educators 13. Plans for establishing, implementing, or evaluating electronic performance support systems 14. Plans for evaluating the success of the electronic training program 15. Plans for evaluating worker performance before and after the training intervention 16. Plans for evaluating the success of the learning technology 17. Plans for managing vendors, contingent workers, or outsourcing agents 18. Plans for meeting instructional objectives 19. Plans for reducing resistance to interventions	**Plans that** • are comprehensive and practical • include measurable milestones for targeted goals (both quantitative and qualitative) • incorporate the best thinking of all business units • are integrated with the organization's plans, mission, vision, and strategies • reflect knowledge of the learner's needs • are supported by individuals that they affect.

Outputs	Quality Requirements
20. Proposals to management, vendors, or clients (written or oral)	**Proposals that** • include all relevant details • include a reasonable amount of information • are well organized and thought out • give the reader an adequate amount of background knowledge • include a due date for responses.
21. Recommendations on learning objectives for training programs 22. Recommendations for improving the effectiveness of learning technologies 23. Recommendations on the most appropriate vendor to provide service 24. Recommendations on which distribution method(s) to select 25. Recommendations on which instructional method(s) to select 26. Recommendations on which presentation method(s) to select	**Recommendations that** • address discrepancies between existing and desired performance • are accompanied by supporting data and rationales • address organizational or individual priorities • address the needs and concerns of the intended audience • are clearly described and easily understood • include multiple options and identify advantages and disadvantages of each option • recognize the reader's perspective • accurately identify problems and opportunities • are tied to the business strategy and organizational goals.
27. Relationships with clients, stakeholders, and decision makers 28. Relationships with learners 29. Relationships with vendors	**Relationships that** • show an appreciation for diversity • recognize individual preferences • are characterized by personal responsibility and self-direction • protect confidentiality • deal effectively with differences in perspective • are effective in meeting personal and organizational goals • are mutually beneficial • are positive • promote personal and professional growth.
30. Reports on content analysis 31. Reports on costs and benefits for learning technologies 32. Reports on needs analysis 33. Reports on resource acquisition and allocation for learning 34. Reports on the cost, benefit, and ROI for training programs 35. Reports on the success of training programs that use learning technologies 36. Reports to learners on their performance 37. Reports to management about employee performance 38. Reports to work groups or teams about their performance	**Reports that** • cite their sources • are clearly written and easily understood • are completed in a timely fashion • contain an executive summary • draw accurate implications, conclusions, and recommendations from data collected • identify limitations and constraints • meet the needs of the intended audience while maintaining research standards • present sufficient data from which to draw conclusions • provide recommendations for implementation • are relevant and sufficient • are technically accurate.

Outputs	Quality Requirements

39. Software for training applications

Software that
- runs on all systems that the organization uses
- is easily revised
- clearly communicates information
- complements the design objectives
- enhances the learning process
- is grammatically accurate
- is interactive
- maintains learner interest
- is maintained and updated
- meets the learner's and the organization's needs
- is relevant to the course content
- respects copyrights and trademarks
- is user friendly.

---

40. Specifications for purchasing hardware and software
41. Specifications for user-friendly facilities and equipment

Specifications that
- account for short- and long-term needs
- are accurate and complete
- are appropriate for the level of need
- are clear and understandable
- include objective evaluation criteria
- meet budgetary restrictions and requirements
- meet learner, instructor, and organizational needs
- are reliable, compatible, and serviceable.

---

42. Storyboards and design documents

Storyboards and design documents that
- are accurate and complete
- are easily revised
- clearly communicate information or concepts
- complement the design objectives
- enhance the learning process
- are grammatically accurate
- are interactive
- maintain learner interest
- are maintained and updated
- meet the learner's needs
- provide good value to the organization
- provide a summary for the learner
- are relevant to the course content
- respect copyrights and trademarks
- are user friendly.

---

43. Support systems that handle the logistical arrangements for the learner
44. Support systems that track and compare actual performance to ideal performance

Support systems that
- include all of the necessary information
- supply information in a timely manner
- are cost-effective for the organization
- meet the learner's, instructor's and organization's expectations
- address the learner's logistical questions in an appropriate manner.

Outputs	Quality Requirements
45. Training programs	**Training programs that** • increase learning efficiency • are cost-effective and valuable to the client • distribute content to a large number of learners synchronously or asynchronously • include effective sound and graphics • give the learner access to coaches and subject matter experts • are self-paced • are instructionally sound • are interactive • are job centered • are delivered at an appropriate time for the learner • meet organizational goals and learner needs • mix media to increase learning retention and learner interest • are performance centered • provide individual attention to the learner • provide timely feedback to the learner.

The second column in table 4.2 is a list of skill and knowledge descriptions that help to describe each competency. These descriptions are not intended to be an exhaustive list and really only outline the skill and knowledge descriptions that were found in the literature review. Deciding what skills and types of knowledge make up a competency is a tricky business. For example, the competency "communication" comprises listening skills, writing skills, speaking skills, grammatical skills, and a knowledge of cultural differences in communication styles. At the same time, communication could also be considered a skill description under the competencies "leadership," "buy-in/advocacy," "interpersonal relationship building/collaboration," and many others. Trying to create rigid guidelines for what is a skill/knowledge description versus what is a competency is a fruitless exercise in mental gymnastics. What is important is that HRD professionals understand what types of skills and knowledge they will need to have in order to succeed in certain roles. How they are classified is immaterial.

Table 4.2: Competencies and Skills and Knowledge Descriptions for Learning Technologies

Competency Name and Description	Skills and Knowledge That Make Up the Competency
GENERAL COMPETENCIES	
* Adult Learning: Understanding how adults learn and how they use knowledge, skills, and attitudes.	• understanding of learning styles • understanding of how the end user will solve problems • ability to facilitate self-directed learning • appreciation of the diverse experiences of adult learners
Instructional Design: Using the ISD model (analysis, design, development, delivery, evaluation) for creating adult education classes that fulfill organizational goals.	• understanding of the six phases of the ISD model • understanding of the part that each role plays in the ISD model • understanding of learning styles • gap analysis skills • evaluation skills • design skills • material development skills • implementation and support skills
* Performance Gap Analysis: Performing front-end analysis by comparing actual and ideal performance levels in the workplace. Identifying opportunities and strategies for improving performance.	• gap analysis skills • intervention selection skills • ability to assess the reasonableness of desired performance levels • ability to present findings of analysis • interviewing skills • focus group facilitation skills • statistical analysis skills • ability to write a valid data collection instrument • ability to analyze historical documentation
* Change Management: Helping people adapt to the changes brought on by new technologies and helping them to see the value and benefits of new technologies.	• understanding of organizational goals • understanding of organizational culture • ability to assess human behavior objectively in the workplace • interviewing skills • focus group facilitation skills • ability to analyze historical documentation • understanding of factors of human motivation • ability to discover the root cause of human behavior

Table 4.2: Competencies and Skills and Knowledge Descriptions for Learning Technologies (continued)

Competency Name and Description	Skills and Knowledge That Make Up the Competency
Leadership: Leading, influencing, and coaching others to help them achieve desired results.	• ability to see the big picture • ability to inspire and motivate others • organizational skills • delegation skills • ability to monitor progress toward organizational goals • understanding of the benefits and risks associated with empowering workers • ability to see one's own behavior as an example for others • ability to maintain a clear vision for the organization's future
* Industry Awareness: Understanding the current and future climate of one's company's industry and formulating strategies that respond to that climate.	• knowledge of one's position within the industry • knowledge of competition's position within the industry • understanding of what future forces are affecting your industry • understanding of competition that exists outside the normal bounds of one's industry • ability to create strategies and contingency plans that allow the organization to have a competitive advantage in this environment
* Buy-in/Advocacy: Building ownership and support for workplace initiatives.	• negotiation skills • verbal, written, and nonverbal communication skills • ability to understand clearly the subject that is being advocated
* Interpersonal Relationship Building/Collaboration: Effectively interacting with others in order to produce meaningful outcomes.	• ability to assess accurately other people's needs • understanding of other people's goals and objectives • understanding of the informal structure of an organization and the demands that it places on individuals • ability to respect other people's values • verbal, nonverbal, and written communication skills
Consulting: Helping clients and stakeholders to question their assumptions, determine their needs, and plan implementation strategies for achieving their goals.	• listening skills • understanding of stakeholder concerns • analytical skills • ability to maintain confidentiality • presentation skills

Competency Name and Description	Skills and Knowledge That Make Up the Competency
* Business Knowledge: Demonstrating awareness of business functions and how business decisions affect financial and nonfinancial work results.	• ability to see the big picture • understanding of how each section of the business interrelates • understanding of the corporation's financial resources and limitations • understanding of the various processes that drive the business • understanding of the types of individuals who work within this business • understanding of the history of the business • understanding of the likely future of the business
Systems Thinking: Recognizing the interrelationship among the driving forces that connect seemingly isolated incidents within the organization. Also taking a holistic view of performance problems in order to find the root causes.	• ability to recognize patterns among events • ability to analyze cause-and-effect relationships accurately • research skills
Contracting: Negotiating, organizing, preparing, monitoring, and evaluating work performed by vendors and consultants.	• consensus-building skills • compromising skills • communication skills • ability to write contracts and requests for proposals • ability to analyze and assess vendor proposals • ability to maintain accurate records • ability to monitor compliance to contract specifications
Project Management: Assessing, planning, negotiating, organizing, monitoring, and evaluating the delivery process. Effectively managing human, capital, and financial resources.	• budgeting skills • organizational skills • ROI skills • scheduling skills • planning skills • consensus-building skills • ability to work on a team • verbal, nonverbal, and written communication skills • research skills • ability to assess ideas and determine their relevance to the project objectively
* Awareness of Learning Technology Industry: Having a general understanding of trends within the learning technology industry and knowing the existing and emerging technologies.	• understanding of the history of the industry • knowledge of the current and emerging trends • knowledge of the current limitations of certain types of technology • cost/benefit analysis skills • networking skills • knowledge of vendors and their standing in the industry • ability to understand the practical application of each technology's features

Table 4.2: Competencies and Skills and Knowledge Descriptions for Learning Technologies (continued)

Competency Name and Description	Skills and Knowledge That Make Up the Competency
* Communication: Applying effective verbal, nonverbal, and written communication methods to achieve desired results.	• writing skills • knowledge of proper grammar • listening skills • speaking skills • nonverbal skills (such as gestures) • knowledge of individuals' differences in communication styles • knowledge of cultural differences in communication styles • understanding of the barriers to effective communication
Program Evaluation: Measuring the success of learning interventions.	• knowledge of statistics • survey instrument design skills • understanding of the four levels of evaluation • knowledge of the various types of measurement • ability to determine what is/and what is not important to measure • ability to evaluate the program within the broader context of organizational goals
Design and Development: Deciding which combination of instructional methods, presentation methods, and distribution methods will best deliver the final program to the learner. Outlining and creating instructional materials that are suitable for electronic dissemination.	• ability to create a design document • ability to create electronic course materials • ability to select instructional, presentation, and distribution methods • ability to understand distribution methods • graphic design skills • HTML design skills • knowledge of performance objectives • programming/authoring skills • resources identification skills • storyboarding skills
Implementation and Support: Coordinating the installation and maintenance of learning technologies.	• presentation skills • ability to understand distribution methods • ability to set up and use electronic software and hardware • ability to diagnose problems that learners experience with the technologies • ability to coordinate assignments with the technical staff • understanding of design specifications of the hardware and software • ability to monitor the effectiveness of the hardware and software

Competency Name and Description	Skills and Knowledge That Make Up the Competency
MANAGEMENT COMPETENCIES	
Management of Learning Technology Selection: Supervising the selection of learning technologies and assuring that these selections meet organizational needs. Determining when, how, and where learning technologies should be used and monitoring the progress of all the other roles in the delivery process.	• budgeting skills • needs assessment skills • knowledge of instructional design • knowledge of programming/authoring tools • resources identification skills • technology evaluation skills • benchmarking skills • balancing electronic and nonelectronic instructional methodologies • knowledge of learner's needs • knowledge of organizational needs • knowledge of instructor's needs
Management of Learning Technology Design and Development: Supervising and assuring the effective integration of performance objectives, course materials, and learning technologies into a design document that fulfills the organization's goals.	• knowledge of graphic design • knowledge of HTML design skills • knowledge of programming/authoring tools • resources identification skills • benchmarking skills • knowledge of storyboarding
Management of Learning Technology Implementation, Support, and Evaluation: Supervising the installation and maintenance of learning technologies and assuring that all systems continuously meet company specifications.	• knowledge of learner's needs • knowledge of organizational needs • knowledge of instructor's needs • ROI analysis skills
DISTRIBUTION METHOD COMPETENCIES	
* Cost Analysis/ROI of the Distribution Methods: Understanding the relative costs of each distribution method, or combination of methods, and assuring that the organization is receiving a good value for the dollars spent on these technologies.	• analysis skills • ability to compare features of various products and evaluate them against organizational needs • understanding of how learners interact with the distribution methods • knowledge of the organization's existing technology infrastructure • knowledge of the current cost for delivering training via various media

Table 4.2: Competencies and Skills and Knowledge Descriptions for Learning Technologies (continued)

Competency Name and Description	Skills and Knowledge That Make Up the Competency
Limitations and Benefits of the Distribution Methods: Knowing the true capabilities of each distribution method, or combination of methods, and tying these capabilities in with the needs of the organization.	• technology evaluation skills • ability to understand distribution methods • understanding of the total cost of implementing new technologies including salaries, lost productivity, rework, and so on • ability to compare actual performance of the technologies to the design specifications • knowledge of the organization's technology infrastructure • understanding of compatibility issues with existing technology
* Effect of Distribution Method on Learners: Assessing how various distribution methods, or combination of methods, will cater to individual learning styles. Balancing learner needs against organizational needs.	• knowledge of adult learning styles • knowledge of learner needs • knowledge of organizational needs
Integration of Distribution Methods: Mixing distribution methods in an effective and efficient manner to facilitate learning.	• knowledge of how various technologies can be combined to deliver training • knowledge of adult learning styles • knowledge of learner needs • knowledge of organizational needs • understanding of the costs associated with each technology • knowledge of the technical abilities of each technology
Remote Site Coordination: Coordinating the installation and maintenance of distribution technologies at a remote site and assuring that all systems continuously meet design specifications.	• understanding of the logistics involved in setting up and supporting the remote site • understanding of the costs involved in operating the remote site • knowledge of adult learning styles • knowledge of learner needs • knowledge of organizational needs • understanding of design specifications of each technology being used
Technology Evaluation: Assuring that all component technologies continuously meet technical design and performance specifications.	• technology evaluation skills • ability to understand distribution methods • knowledge of adult learning styles • knowledge of learner needs • knowledge of organizational needs • understanding of design specifications of each technology being used

Competency Name and Description	Skills and Knowledge That Make Up the Competency

PRESENTATION METHOD COMPETENCIES

* Cost Analysis/ROI of the Presentation Methods:

Understanding the relative costs of each presentation method, or combination of methods, and assuring that the organization is receiving a good value for the dollars spent on these technologies.

- analysis skills
- ability to compare features of various products and evaluate them against organizational needs
- understanding of how learners interact with the various presentation methods
- knowledge of which distribution method can deliver which presentation formats
- knowledge of the current cost for delivering training via various media

---

Limitations and Benefits of the Presentation Method:

Knowing the true capabilities of each presentation method, or combination of methods, and tying these capabilities in with the needs of the organization.

- understanding of the costs associated with each technology
- ability to assess the relevance of design specifications towards meeting organizational goals
- ability to compare features and limitations among various technologies
- knowledge of the organization's technology infrastructure
- understanding of compatibility issues with existing technology
- knowledge of adult learning styles
- knowledge of learner needs
- knowledge of organizational needs

Effect of Presentation Method on Learners:

Assessing how various presentation methods, or combination of methods, will cater to individual learning styles. Balancing learner needs against organizational needs.

- knowledge of adult learning styles
- knowledge of learner needs
- knowledge of organizational needs

Integration of Presentation Methods:

Mixing presentation methods in an effective and efficient manner to facilitate learning.

- knowledge of how various presentation methods can be combined to enhance the learning experience
- knowledge of adult learning styles
- knowledge of learner needs
- knowledge of organizational needs
- understanding of the costs associated with each presentation method
- understanding of which distribution methods can be used to deliver the various presentation methods
- knowledge of how various technologies can be combined to deliver training
- knowledge of the organization's technology infrastructure
- knowledge of learner access to the various distribution methods

Roles for Learning Technologies

The ability to decide on and use an emerging array of learning technologies in a variety of roles is rapidly becoming a key set of required competencies for HRD professionals. Whether the HRD function is training, human performance improvement, or something else, it is increasingly evident that HRD departments must have staff members who are capable of using learning technologies for training and development. These capabilities ensure that the department can perform tasks ranging from advising on technology systems acquisition to designing and using specific technology applications to providing the logistical support often required for technology-based delivery. The training team must play a role in all of these activities, as well as in the design, development, and delivery of training using whatever technology mix is appropriate. It cannot be overemphasized that all of this is assuming that training has already been determined to be the appropriate intervention for solving the performance problem.

While past ASTD studies have identified 15 roles that HRD professionals might play (11 in McLagan, 1989 and four in Rothwell, 1996), not all of them relate directly to the use of learning technologies. For this study, there are eight major roles that play a part in the selection and use of learning technologies (see table 4.3). In most instances, the broad range of roles required to select, manage, and use learning technologies probably will not be represented by a single HRD staff member. While a few individuals may become "learning technology specialists," it is more likely that existing roles within the HRD department will take on the additional responsibilities of implementing learning technologies.

The use of roles should not imply that this is a linear process, where one person simply "hands off" to another. An effective learning technology strategy requires ongoing collaborative input from a team of internal and external sources.

Relationship Between Roles and Competencies

Table 4.4 shows which competencies apply to which roles. To create this table, researchers asked respondents to rate the relevance of each competency to each role (see page 28 for the survey instrument layout). Only those role-to-competency correlations that had a mean score of 2.0 or higher were determined to be "important" or "very important" to the role.

Table 4.3: Roles for Learning Technologies

Roles	Description of the Role
HRD Manager	Determines which learning technology, or combination of technologies, an organization should use to meet the comprehensive needs of the company. Decides when these technologies should be used and monitors the progress of all the other roles in the delivery process.
Analyst	Identifies performance gaps and recommends performance objectives that address the gaps. Determines if training is the proper intervention.
Designer	Determines what content, instructional methods, presentation methods, and distribution methods will achieve the desired objectives and will suit the needs of the trainee population. Also creates the design document that will integrate all of these elements.
Developer	Uses the design document to create materials that are delivered via various presentation methods.
Implementor	Works with technical staff to set up and provide logistical support for technology devices. Also works with suppliers to produce and distribute electronic training materials.
Instructor	Facilitates learning in either a live broadcast or in an advanced technology classroom.
Evaluator	Measures the success of the course objectives and the effectiveness of the technology.
Organizational Change Agent	Helps the organization adapt to the new technology and see its value and benefits.

Table 4.4: Roles and Competencies

General Competencies	HRD Manager	Analyst	Designer	Developer	Imple-mentor	Instructor	Evaluator	Change Agent
	Competency Names							
Adult Learning	✔	✔	✔	✔		✔	✔	
Instructional Design		✔	✔	✔			✔	
Performance Gap Analysis	✔	✔	✔				✔	✔
Change Management	✔	✔			✔	✔		✔
Leadership	✔				✔	✔		✔
Industry Awareness	✔	✔	✔		✔			✔
Buy-in/Advocacy	✔	✔			✔	✔		✔
Interpersonal Relationship Building/Collaboration	✔	✔	✔	✔	✔	✔		✔
Consulting	✔	✔			✔			✔
Business Knowledge	✔	✔	✔		✔			✔
Systems Thinking	✔	✔	✔					✔
Contracting	✔							
Project Management	✔	✔						✔
Awareness of Learning Technology Industry	✔	✔	✔	✔				✔
Communication	✔	✔	✔	✔	✔	✔	✔	✔
Program Evaluation	✔	✔					✔	✔
Design and Development		✔	✔	✔				
Implementation and Support					✔			

Management Competencies	Competency Names							
	HRD Manager	Analyst	Designer	Developer	Imple-mentor	Instructor	Evaluator	Change Agent
Management of Learning Technology Selection	✔	✔	✔					
Management of Learning Technology Design and Development	✔	✔	✔	✔				
Management of Learning Technology Implementation, Support, and Evaluation	✔				✔			

Distribution Method Competencies	Competency Names							
Cost Analysis/ROI of the Distribution Methods	✔	✔	✔				✔	✔
Limitations and Benefits of the Distribution Methods	✔	✔	✔	✔				
Effect of Distribution Method on Learners	✔	✔	✔	✔			✔	
Integration of Distribution Methods		✔	✔	✔				
Remote Site Coordination					✔			
Technology Evaluation					✔		✔	

Presentation Method Competencies	Competency Names							
Cost Analysis/ROI of the Presentation Methods	✔	✔	✔				✔	✔
Limitations and Benefits of the Presentation Methods	✔	✔	✔	✔				
Effect of Presentation Method on Learners		✔	✔	✔		✔		
Integration of Presentation Methods		✔	✔	✔		✔		

The Relationship Among Roles, Competencies, and Outputs

All of the above data is only useful if readers can understand the relationship among roles, competencies, and outputs. Table 4.5 gives a broad picture of how all of this information interrelates. It is important to understand that this is a static snapshot of where the profession is today and will be in the near future. As technologies and professional roles change, many of these relationships may cease to be relevant. At the same time, having a basis for understanding "who produces what and how they produce it" is a valuable foundation for the future.

Competencies and outputs will be repeated for each role that they apply to. In general, competencies are likely to apply to numerous roles, while outputs will apply to a limited number of roles. This makes sense considering how work gets done in an organization. For instance, a report (which is prepared for executives) might be the product of an HRD manager. At the same time, there may be many contributing reports that were prepared by an analyst, an evaluator, or an organizational change agent for the HRD manager. The point here is that there should be some overlap in roles that produce certain outputs, but not too much overlap. Similarly, it is likely that many people within the HRD department will possess certain basic competencies, although their levels of mastery will vary.

Table 4.5: Master Table of Roles, Competencies, and Outputs

Roles	Competencies	Outputs
HRD Manager	<ul><li>Adult Learning</li><li>Performance Gap Analysis</li><li>Change Management</li><li>Leadership</li><li>Industry Awareness</li><li>Buy-in/Advocacy</li><li>Interpersonal Relationship Building/Collaboration</li><li>Consulting</li><li>Business Knowledge</li><li>Systems Thinking</li><li>Contracting</li><li>Project Management</li><li>Awareness of Learning Technology Industry</li><li>Communication</li><li>Program Evaluation</li><li>Management of Learning Technology Selection</li><li>Management of Learning Technology Design and Development</li><li>Management of Learning Technology Implementation, Support, and Evaluation</li><li>Cost Analysis/ROI of the Distribution Methods</li><li>Limitations and Benefits of the Distribution Methods</li><li>Effect of Distribution Method on Learners</li></ul>	<ul><li>Contracts for vendors to provide service</li><li>Contracts or agreements with management, clients (written or oral)</li><li>Guidelines for designers and developers</li><li>Guidelines for instructors and facilitators</li><li>Guidelines for needs analysts and evaluators</li><li>Plans for choosing effective and efficient technology</li><li>Plans for converting classroom instructors into distance learning educators</li><li>Plans for establishing, implementing, or evaluating electronic performance support systems</li><li>Plans for evaluating the success of the electronic training program</li><li>Plans for evaluating worker performance before and after the training intervention</li><li>Plans for evaluating the success of the learning technology</li><li>Plans for managing vendors, contingent workers, or outsourcing agents</li><li>Plans for meeting instructional objectives</li><li>Plans for reducing resistance to interventions</li><li>Proposals to management, vendors, or clients (written or oral)</li></ul>

Roles	Competencies	Outputs
HRD Manager, *continued*	• Cost Analysis/ROI of the Presentation Methods • Limitations and Benefits of the Presentation Methods	• Recommendations on learning objectives for training programs • Recommendations for improving the effectiveness of learning technologies • Recommendations on the most appropriate vendor to provide service • Relationships with clients, stakeholders, and decision makers • Relationships with vendors • Reports on resource acquisition and allocation for learning technologies • Reports to management about employee performance • Reports to work groups or teams about their performance • Specifications for purchasing hardware and software • Specifications for user-friendly facilities and equipment • Training programs
Analyst	• Adult Learning • Instructional Design • Performance Gap Analysis • Change Management • Industry Awareness • Buy-in/Advocacy • Interpersonal Relationship Building/Collaboration • Consulting • Business Knowledge • Systems Thinking • Project Management • Awareness of Learning Technology Industry • Communication • Program Evaluation • Design and Development • Management of Learning Technology Selection • Management of Learning Technology Design and Development • Cost Analysis/ROI of the Distribution Methods • Limitations and Benefits of the Distribution Methods • Effect of Distribution Method on Learners • Integration of Distribution Methods • Cost Analysis/ROI of the Presentation Methods	• Recommendations on learning objectives for training programs • Recommendations on the most appropriate vendor to provide service • Reports on costs and benefits for learning technologies • Reports on needs analysis • Reports on the cost, benefit, and ROI for training programs

Table 4.5: Master Table of Roles, Competencies, and Outputs (continued)

Roles	Competencies	Outputs
Analyst, *continued*	• Limitations and Benefits of the Presentation Methods • Effect of Presentation Method on Learners • Integration of Presentation Methods	
Designer	• Adult Learning • Instructional Design • Performance Gap Analysis • Industry Awareness • Interpersonal Relationship Building/Collaboration • Business Knowledge • Systems Thinking • Awareness of Learning Technology Industry • Communication • Design and Development • Management of Learning Technology Selection • Management of Learning Technology Design and Development • Cost Analysis/ROI of the Distribution Methods • Limitations and Benefits of the Distribution Methods • Effect of Distribution Method on Learners • Integration of Distribution Methods • Cost Analysis/ROI of the Presentation Methods • Limitations and Benefits of the Presentation Methods • Effect of Presentation Method on Learners • Integration of Presentation Methods	• Classroom environments • Equipment for learning • Recommendations on the most appropriate vendor to provide service • Recommendations on which distribution method(s) to select • Recommendations on which instructional method(s) to select • Recommendations on which presentation method(s) to select • Storyboards and design documents • Training programs

Roles	Competencies	Outputs
Developer	• Adult Learning • Instructional Design • Interpersonal Relationship Building/Collaboration • Awareness of Learning Technology Industry • Communication • Design and Development • Management of Learning Technology Design and Development • Limitations and Benefits of the Distribution Methods • Effect of Distribution Method on Learners • Integration of Distribution Methods • Limitations and Benefits of the Presentation Methods • Effect of Presentation Method on Learners • Integration of Presentation Methods	• Classroom environments • Materials for the student (electronic and paper-based) • Software for training applications
Implementor	• Change Management • Leadership • Industry Awareness • Buy-in/Advocacy • Interpersonal Relationship Building/Collaboration • Consulting • Business Knowledge • Communication • Implementation and Support • Management of Learning Technology Implementation, Support, and Evaluation • Remote Site Coordination • Technology Evaluation	• Classroom environments • Communication systems • Equipment for learning • Support systems that handle the logistical arrangements for the learner
Instructor	• Adult Learning • Change Management • Leadership • Buy-in/Advocacy • Interpersonal Relationship Building/Collaboration • Communication • Effect of Presentation Method on Learners • Integration of Presentation Methods	• Classroom environments • Relationships with learners

Table 4.5: Master Table of Roles, Competencies, and Outputs (continued)

Roles	Competencies	Outputs
Evaluator	• Adult Learning • Instructional Design • Performance Gap Analysis • Communication • Program Evaluation • Cost Analysis/ROI of the Distribution Methods • Effect of Distribution Method on Learners • Technology Evaluation • Cost Analysis/ROI of the Presentation Methods	• Evaluation instruments • Recommendations for improving the effectiveness of learning technologies • Reports on content analysis • Reports on the cost, benefit, and ROI for training programs • Reports on the success of training programs that use learning technologies • Reports to learners on their performance • Reports to management about employee performance • Reports to work groups or teams about their performance • Support systems that track and compare actual performance to ideal performance • Training programs
Organizational Change Agent	• Performance Gap Analysis • Change Management • Leadership • Industry Awareness • Buy-in/Advocacy • Interpersonal Relationship Building/Collaboration • Consulting • Business Knowledge • Systems Thinking • Project Management • Awareness of Learning Technology Industry • Communication • Program Evaluation • Cost Analysis/ROI of the Distribution Methods • Cost Analysis/ROI of the Presentation Methods	• Relationships with clients, stakeholders, and decision makers • Relationships with learners • Reports to learners on their performance • Reports to management about employee performance • Reports to work groups or teams about their performance

SECTION 5   THE ETHICS OF USING TECHNOLOGY FOR LEARNING PURPOSES
By George M. Piskurich

In her *Models for HRD Practice* competency study, McLagan detailed 13 major ethical issues associated with HRD work that may arise as that work is being accomplished:

1. Maintaining appropriate confidentiality
2. Saying "no" to inappropriate requests
3. Showing respect for copyrights, sources, and intellectual property
4. Ensuring truth in claims, data, and recommendations
5. Balancing organizational and individual needs and interests
6. Ensuring customer and user involvement, participation, and ownership
7. Avoiding conflicts of interest
8. Managing personal biases
9. Showing respect for, interest in, and representation of individual and population differences
10. Making the intervention appropriate to the customer's or user's needs
11. Being sensitive to the direct and indirect effects of intervention and acting to address negative consequences
12. Pricing or costing products or services fairly
13. Using power appropriately

Odin Westgaard's *A Credo for Performance Technologists*[1] reaffirms McLagan's ideas. In his credo he notes that professional performance improvement work should not

◆ violate professional, academic, or business ethics with such less-than-honest billing practices as submitting low bids, but higher final bills
◆ promise that solutions will work when they may not
◆ make false claims regarding return on investment
◆ use client information for personal gain
◆ falsify data
◆ compromise human performance improvement for personal or political gain by providing interventions that are acceptable to the client but ill-suited to the context
◆ take credit for another person's work
◆ make false claims about another person's behaviors or potential accomplishments.

These same ethical standards apply to the practitioner of learning. By considering the following factors, it is easy to see the connection between HRD work, performance improvement work, and the application of learning technologies:

---

[1] *A Credo for Performance Technologists.* Westgaard, O., 1988.

◆ Technology gives us broad access to confidential resources that must be guarded judiciously.
◆ Using technology ethically requires us to say no when the request is not appropriate.
◆ Respect for copyrights, sources, and intellectual property has been and continues to be a major issue when technology makes it so easy to "just borrow" material.
◆ Being truthful in what we claim technology will do is mandatory if we are going to continue to be believed by those who trust us to recommend wisely.
◆ Pricing or costing fairly when dealing with the large sums technology requires is paramount.

In *ASTD Models for Human Performance Improvement*, Rothwell uses Westgaard's credo to develop a checklist comparing ethical issues to the roles of performance improvement. A few changes can make it a checklist for learning technology as well:

◆ Maintaining an objective stance when examining and verifying the results of a process
◆ Taking responsibility for the impact of their work on other people
◆ Maintaining professional, academic, and business ethics by ensuring that final bills match original work bids
◆ Making realistic claims to clients about the impact of technology-based interventions or strategies
◆ Making realistic claims about the return on investment of interventions
◆ Maintaining client confidentiality, using information only to help the client and not for personal gain
◆ Ensuring that data are accurate, reliable, and valid and are never falsified
◆ Taking credit for one's own work only
◆ Providing accurate information about the behaviors or potential accomplishments of other people—and avoiding false claims about the behaviors or accomplishments of others
◆ Encouraging and modeling consistent application of policies
◆ Preserving employees' rights and safety
◆ Maintaining compliance with applicable laws, rules, and regulations
◆ Accurately representing oneself and one's technology intervention processes and results
◆ Providing adequate information to other people

There are some additional ethical considerations that apply to the use of any electronic medium. Such issues include intellectual property, privacy, and censorship.

Intellectual Property: Since electronic data is so easy to access and reproduce, there is an increased tendency to circumvent the normal copyright guidelines. It is essential that practitioners avoid this temptation and respect the rights of the original author(s). This is not as easy as it may sound. Much of the material that is available electronically (particularly on the Internet) has been "recirculated" numerous times. Anyone who has received the same joke several times from several different sources in their e-mail in-box can attest to this fact. As in art, there is a tendency to believe that all creative works are merely the continuation of work that has gone before. While this is true in many circumstances, each artist or author still deserves the credit (and possible compensation) for the role that he or she played in this creative process. For this reason, it is important to invest sincere effort in locating the original authors and gaining their permission to use their material.

Privacy: The ease of transmitting digital information is a double-edged sword. While there are tremendous benefits to having limitless information, there is a greater risk of invasion of privacy than at any time in history. In today's world, the right set of passwords could entitle an intruder to all of a person's medical, financial, and social information. All of the encryption technology in the world won't change the fact that respect for privacy must be at the center of this issue. Without this respect, the digital world will remain an exciting but perilous place to live.

Censorship: The ethical dilemma over censorship existed long before the advent of electronic technologies. But in a world where unlimited information is available in just a few key strokes, this issue takes on new dimensions. The 1995 Communications Decency Act sought to limit the transmission of material that is deemed to be socially unacceptable. This act has reignited the debate between individual rights versus societal rights. Furthermore, it has raised the issue of what decency is and when is it acceptable (for example, between consenting adults) or not acceptable (for example, when children can access it). While there are no easy answers to this dilemma, it is important to realize that censorship should not be taken lightly. The good of the individual versus the good of the organization must always be considered in a delicate balance.

There are numerous resources available that spell out the specifics of computer ethics. One good source is the British Computer Society's Web page (http://www.ccsr.cms.dmu.ac.uk/codes/Bcs.html). With their permission, we have reproduced their Code of Conduct, which they adopted in April 1992. While they are not specifically referring to learning technology practitioners, the same rules apply.

Code of Conduct (April 22nd, 1992)

Rules of Professional Conduct [2]
As an aid to understanding, these rules have been grouped into the principal duties which all members should endeavor to discharge in pursuing their professional lives.

The Public Interest
1. Members shall in their professional practice safeguard public health and safety and have regard to protection of the environment.
2. Members shall have due regard to the legitimate rights of third parties.
3. Members shall ensure that within their chosen fields they have knowledge and understanding of relevant legislation, regulations and standards and that they comply with such requirements.
4. Members shall in their professional practice have regard to basic human rights and shall avoid any actions that adversely affect such rights.

Duty to Employers and Clients
5. Members shall carry out work with due care and diligence in accordance with the requirements of the employer or client and shall, if their professional judgment is overruled, indicate the likely consequences.
6. Members shall endeavor to complete work undertaken on time and to budget and shall advise their employer or client as soon as practicable if any overrun is foreseen.

---

[2] Reprinted by permission of the British Computer Society.

7. Members shall not offer or provide, or receive in return, any inducement for the introduction of business from a client unless there is full prior disclosure of the facts to that client.

8. Members shall not disclose or authorize, to be disclosed, or use for personal gain or to benefit a third party, confidential information acquired in the course of professional practice, except with prior, written permission of the employer or client, or at the direction of a court of law.

9. Members should seek to avoid being put in a position where they may become privy to or party to activities or information concerning activities which would conflict with their responsibilities in 1-4 above.

10. Members shall not misrepresent or withhold information on the capabilities of products, systems or services with which they are concerned or take advantage of the lack of knowledge or inexperience of others.

11. Members shall not, except where specifically so instructed, handle client's monies or place contracts or orders in connection with work on which they are engaged when acting as an independent consultant.

12. Members shall not purport to exercise independent judgment on behalf of a client on any product or service in which they knowingly have any interest, financial or otherwise.

Duty to the Profession

13. Members shall uphold the reputation of the Profession and shall seek to improve professional standards through participation in their development, use and enforcement, and shall avoid any action which will adversely affect the good standing of the Profession.

14. Members shall in their professional practice seek to advance public knowledge and understanding of computing and information systems and technology and to counter false or misleading statements which are detrimental to the Profession.

15. Members shall encourage and support fellow members in their professional development and, where possible, provide opportunities for the professional development of new entrants to the Profession.

16. Members shall act with integrity towards fellow members and to members of other professions with whom they are concerned in a professional capacity and shall avoid engaging in any activity which is incompatible with professional status.

17. Members shall not make any public statement in their professional capacity unless properly qualified and, where appropriate, authorized to do so, and shall have due regard to the likely consequences of any such statement on others.

Professional Competence and Integrity

18. Members shall seek to upgrade their professional knowledge and skill and shall maintain awareness of technological developments, procedures and standards which are relevant to their field, and shall encourage their subordinates to do likewise.

19. Members shall seek to conform to recognized good practice including quality standards which are in their judgment relevant, and shall encourage their subordinates to do likewise.

20. Members shall only offer to do work or provide service which is within their professional competence and shall not lay claim to any level of competence which they do not possess, and any professional opinion which they are asked to give shall be objective and reliable.

21. Members shall accept professional responsibility for their work and for the work of subordinates and associates under their direction, and shall not terminate any assignment except for good reason and on reasonable notice.

22. Members shall avoid any situation that may give rise to a conflict of interest between themselves and their client and shall make full and immediate disclosure to the client if any such conflict should occur.

SECTION 6 SUGGESTED AUDIENCES FOR AND USES OF THIS STUDY
By George M. Piskurich

Technology has a different effect on individual roles within the profession. Therefore, the audiences for and uses of this study are somewhat varied. For purposes of this study, we will divide the suggested audience into four categories: practitioners, managers, academicians, and others.

Practitioners

Practitioners are people who use learning technologies for training and development, organization development, performance improvement activities, or a combination of the three.

This includes those who use learning technologies intermittently in their jobs, as well as those who focus on using learning technologies. This book can be an important resource to guide their work and development. Practitioners' uses include the following:

◆ **Designing jobs:** Practitioners may use this book to help describe or design their jobs. The lists of future forces, outputs, competencies, and quality requirements may be used as menus from which to select items relevant to a job. Practitioners may create a job description by combining one or more role profiles. People may stretch into roles that are defined here, or they may add challenge and opportunity to their individual development by including roles and outputs that require new competencies. This book gives practitioners a place to begin when identifying new roles that will help them in their career. It also describes how to assess, through various tools, their current competence level.

◆ **Managing performance:** This book can be a valuable tool to help guide performance. It can be the basis for both goals and feedback. For goal setting, the future forces provide initial ideas. Individuals can identify the future forces likely to have the most impact on their jobs during a performance period. This helps set the context for selecting priorities. Individuals may supplement the listed items with other forces that may be important for their specific jobs or organization. Improving the feedback performers receive can be one of the most powerful interventions. By using the roles, competencies, and outputs described here as a reference point, people who do technology work have the basis for soliciting specific, concrete, and timely feedback from customers and other stakeholders about their performance. This can lead to continuous improvement in their own performance. People who set goals this way and confirm them with their managers, colleagues, and customers will have a good basis for later feedback discussions and performance evaluation. The key evaluation question will be "To what extent did outputs meet the quality requirements?"

◆ **Planning careers:** This book provides a broad picture of the learning technology field. People can envision themselves in that moving picture as it looks today and will look tomorrow. Key career planning questions to answer include the following:

1. "What future forces will I face as my career develops?"
2. "Which forces do I want to respond to?"
3. "What roles do I want to perform?"
4. "What competencies will I need to develop in order to perform these roles?"

◆ **Fostering professional development:** Technologies for HRD will continue to develop and change. In what areas do practitioners need to be developed? Using this book, practitioners can examine their professional development needs to identify areas in which they may need to increase or deepen their knowledge. Better ways of working are sure to evolve because every person who uses technology is growing and changing. Jobs will be different in the next year (and in two, five, and 10 years) partly because individuals will make them different. In such a change-filled scenario, development could be haphazard, but it doesn't need to be. This book provides tools for planning and guiding the development of technology-related competencies so people can anticipate their own needs and keep themselves prepared.

◆ **Documenting accomplishments:** This book begins to provide the basis for a common technology language. By documenting work accomplishments in terms of the roles, competencies, and outputs described here, practitioners can show what they have accomplished. This can be helpful in communicating needs and outcomes. Such a common language is particularly important as technology becomes more common and obtainable for more people. A key question that often arises for individuals is, "What quality of work are you capable of?" In some professions, third parties offer programs that certify individuals' performance capabilities. Currently, there's no widely accepted certification program for learning technologists. But there's no reason people can't manage and document their own accomplishments and use the results to help them plan performance improvement or sell their ability to make specific HRD contributions.

◆ **Identifying outputs and quality requirements:** This book can help practitioners identify outputs that they want to master. It is highly recommended that practitioners then find a mentor who can help them establish a realistic set of quality requirements to measure their success against.

◆ **Consulting with others:** Technology practitioners are basically consultants, either external or internal. This book can help them adopt new foci for their work. It provides a useful and flexible blueprint to guide consulting engagements in all aspect of technology.

◆ **Maintaining ethical standards:** Maintaining ethical standards is important because some critics claim that too much emphasis on technology dehumanizes people and minimizes the importance of balancing the process with individual and organizational needs. This does not have to be true. People who use technology can be as sensitive to individual needs as they are to the technological needs. This book provides a means to do this.

Managers

HRD managers select, coordinate, and provide support for people who use technology. This book helps support those involved in this management work.

◆ **Designing technology jobs:** An important aspect of a manager's responsibility is designing departments and jobs by deciding how to organize roles and outputs. The lists of roles and outputs here are building blocks of this design. They can help assign roles, outputs, or both to positions or to individuals.

◆ **Staffing:** Staffing is the process of matching people and jobs. Job profiles can help produce these matches. As a first step, managers can identify the major technology roles they will expect a person to perform. Then they can identify which competencies are most important across the roles. These and any additional competencies or personal factors that will be critical to job success can be the basis for job announcements, résumé reviews, and interviews. Managers can look for people who have an appropriate level of expertise in the competencies of the targeted roles. Other aspects of staffing include

1. assessing the competency levels of existing staff
2. managing outsourcing opportunities
3. hiring vendors to assist with any facet of technology deemed a need.

◆ **Assessing and developing staff:** This book is also a tool for staff development. Managers can use it to help develop individual staff members. This involves

1. identifying or clarifying work expectations for those who do technology work
2. assessing their competencies and comparing these management perceptions—and the behavior examples that support those perceptions—with the individuals' self-evaluations
3. helping individual staff members select and commit to developing one or two competencies
4. providing recommendations, resources, and personal coaching and feedback to support their development
5. documenting the accomplishments of people who are involved in technology projects
6. training people to apply technology effectively.

◆ **Managing HRD professional performance:** This book can help individuals and the technology team set goals. To use the book this way, managers may create performance goals by listing the outputs that are most important for the next performance period. Then they can focus feedback and performance review discussions on each output and the indicators or measures of it.

◆ **Preparing for the future:** This is perhaps the most important aspect for a manager of learning technology who must look at the big picture. Managers bear responsibility for setting a direction for their departments or functions. The trends identified in this book provide a starting point for thinking about ways that technology processes can be positioned to anticipate or react to those trends.

◆ **Assuring ethical conduct:** This book can help managers

1. anticipate which ethical issues are likely to arise for themselves and their staff
2. be models of ethical behavior themselves
3. discuss and encourage discussions of ethical challenges in which the right answer is not clear or where there are conflicting needs
4. be careful to avoid indirect encouragement of breaches of ethics (for example, a manager shouldn't make it difficult for staff to say "no" to inappropriate requests or ignore their breaches of copyright)
5. take a clear stand on ethical issues and establish codes of conduct for technology staff and others who work with learning technologies.

Academicians

Many undergraduate and graduate learning technology programs exist in the United States and in other nations. Some are offered for degrees, and some are offered for continuing education credit. Administrators, faculty, and staff working in those programs can use this book as a framework for assessing program needs, planning program enhancements and courses, assessing learners, formulating and implementing research agenda, advising learners enrolled in the programs (or considering enrollment), developing faculty, and evaluating program processes and outcomes.

◆ **Assessing needs:** This book can be a guideline for
1. assessing employers' needs for people who are able to apply technology effectively
2. assessing interests in academic course work among prospective students.
◆ **Planning programs and courses:** This book can be used to
1. identify the competencies, roles, or both that the total curriculum will address
2. list all existing courses that address each role, competency, or both
3. identify roles, competencies, or both that need more emphasis or attention
4. establish new courses or revise old courses based on roles, competencies, and future trends identified here
5. benchmark programs or courses against offerings at other academic institutions.
◆ **Assessing learners:** The book can provide a framework for
1. identifying sources of prospective students;
2. assessing differences between individual student competencies and the competencies required for success in technology work, which can become the basis for individualized plans of study.
◆ **Advising learners:** Students enrolled in academic programs in technology often have individualized needs for advice about what courses to take, what career goals to pursue, and how to build the competencies they need to realize their career goals. This book is a useful tool for organizing such discussions.
◆ **Managing and developing faculty:** Faculty members who teach in academic programs in technology must stay current if they are to teach effectively and provide appropriate guidance to students. This book can be useful for assessing faculty competencies and suggesting professional development activities to build those competencies.

◆ **Evaluating program processes and results:** Accountability is the key word for the 1990s. Just as technology practitioners are under increasing pressure to demonstrate that their efforts lead to payoffs for their organizations, so too are academic programs under pressure to demonstrate that they are delivering effective results. This book can be used as a standard against which to measure academic programs and results.

Line Managers

Line managers bear primary responsibility for serving customers, making products, dealing with suppliers, and meeting distributor needs. In addition, they are often asked to act as facilitators, managers, and evaluators of technology interventions, as well as the troubleshooters when things go wrong. They can use this book to develop a common language to use when advising their colleagues on technology issues, when describing their own needs for technology-based interventions, and when interacting with HRD professionals. This common language facilitates communication across line and staff units and describes the competencies that should be displayed by those who are doing technology work ultimately for the managers and their staffs. This book can also provide information on choosing and facilitating technology-based interventions—tasks that often fall on the manager to a greater or lesser extent.

Information Systems Staff

An important aspect of any technology intervention is the training. However, many of the information systems staff who might directly benefit from understanding training issues find that they have no basis to build upon. This book can help these individuals to see how they might use technology to teach technology more efficiently and learn what skills they will need in order to do this. The same uses that are listed above for the line manager would also apply to the information systems staff.

SECTION 7 CONCLUSION
By Ethan S. Sanders

The preceding pages have supplied a great deal of information on the eight roles, 31 competencies, and 45 outputs that practitioners will need for implementing learning technologies. They have also provided a classification system for the technologies themselves and examined the theoretical underpinnings of this topic. It is very easy to get overwhelmed by so much information. This conclusion will help to synthesize some of the book's main ideas, put them into a meaningful frame of reference, and add some new ideas to consider.

It Takes a Team to Implement Learning Technologies

Throughout this book, the phrase "use, selection, and management of learning technologies" has been repeated many times. While it is easy to put these three items together in a sentence, they represent a broad range of responsibilities and skill levels. It is important for HRD professionals to understand that they cannot effectively implement learning technologies on their own. It is unlikely that even a large staff of HRD professionals will possess all of the technical expertise necessary for implementing these technologies. The technologies are too numerous, change too rapidly, and have too many individual specifications for HRD professionals to try to handle them on their own. Instead, partnerships with members of the technical community (for example, information systems professionals, information technology professionals, and so forth) will be necessary in order to make these learning technologies efficient and effective. When speaking at the Interactive '97 conference in Denver, Lance Dublin[3] said, "The smartest thing a trainer can do today is to make friends with someone in the information systems department." With the information age comes a new age of collaboration and symbiotic relationships. This is one of the most exciting aspects of the technological revolution.

The eight roles that have been presented in this study are more than a convenient grouping of competencies and outputs. They represent the many layers of responsibilities that must exist when dealing with learning technologies. The responsibilities of designers, developers, and implementors are very different than the responsibilities of managers, evaluators, analysts, and organizational change agents. Each of these roles deals with information that is on a very different plane. For instance, decisions HRD managers make regarding selecting technology involve a detailed understanding of the organization's goals, the existing technology infrastructure, budgetary requirements, and external forces. For designers, the considerations are more pragmatic. Designers are usually told which distribution technologies are at their disposal. Therefore, they focus on how to make the most

out of these available resources. To do this requires careful consideration of how each instructional method, presentation method, and available distribution method can be paired in order to create effective learning experiences. For evaluators, analysts, and organizational change agents, the considerations center on the amount of change that these learning interventions are likely to produce. Only through careful measurement can HRD professionals determine what effect these interventions had on the organization. The point is that learning technologies is a dynamic field that requires many roles working at many levels and working in harmony.

It's All About Improving Human Performance

The days of assuming that training is a cure-all for human performance problems have passed. It is essential to remember that training represents only one type of intervention that can be used to improve human performance in the workplace. Only a detailed performance analysis can uncover the root causes for performance problems and begin to shed light on the most effective means for solving these problems. Training is only one of many types of interventions available to today's practitioners. In general, training can be among the most costly, invasive, and time-consuming interventions available. At the same time, there are situations where training is simply the best option. There is a meaningful analogy between performance improvement interventions and medical interventions. Surgery is only one type of medical intervention that medical practitioners can use to help the healing process. Surgical interventions are risky, costly, invasive, and time consuming. At the same time, there are many circumstances where surgery is clearly the proper intervention for solving medical problems. This is an important analogy to remember as learning technologies are implemented in an organization. The benefits of learning technologies can not nullify the need for properly identifying the causes of performance problems.

Once training is determined to be the proper intervention, it should not be a foregone conclusion that learning technologies are the best method for delivering new information. There are many factors

---

[3] *Lance Dublin is the CEO of the Dublin Group, a change implementation and performance consulting organization.*

to consider when choosing among classroom training, electronic delivery of information, job aids, or electronic performance support systems. These factors include the size of the trainee population, the geographical proximity of the audience, the subject matter, the company's resources, the amount of time available for training, and how quickly the information will become outdated.

Classifying Technology and Changing Competencies

Much of this study focused on the classification system of instructional methods, presentation methods, and distribution methods. Although no classification system will be perfect forever, the act of classifying items is important. This classification has created a new paradigm for understanding learning technologies. As new technologies enter the marketplace and new philosophies on learning emerge, it is likely that new distinctions and terms will need to be created. Classification systems such as this force us to assess the relationships between items closely. While this can be challenging, it is the root of understanding complex phenomena.

These same changes in technology will create the need for new competencies. Although certain competencies will likely endure (such as adult learning), others may become outdated. Change and temporariness are inherent in competency studies. The role of people within organizations, the tools they use, and the techniques they rely on are ever changing. Therefore, it is unthinkable that the competencies in this study will remain viable indefinitely. Instead, they will establish a foundation for future studies and allow people to understand the roots of this profession. This study should be viewed as a living document.

Learning Technologies Represent a Dynamic Convergence

One reason that learning technologies can become such a hotly debated issue is that they represent a unique convergence between a sociological phenomenon (learning) and a scientific phenomenon (technology). Because of this, it is challenging to strike a balance between how much the technological issues should be emphasized versus how much the humanistic issues should be emphasized when trying to implement these technologies within an organization. It is easy to become enamored with the incredible features that these new technologies offer. It is also easy to feel threatened by the new technology and to feel that it is replacing the sacred tradition of learning

institutions. This fear is amplified by the fact that learning lies at the heart of what it means to be human. One of the greatest challenges for the learning profession, therefore, is to find what Aristotle referred to as the "middle path." Both the technical implementation issues and the human interaction issues constantly need to be addressed when implementing learning technologies. Section 5 of this book addressed ethics for HRD work and ethics for using technology. While this was a great deal of information, there seems to be a common thread. The ethical implementation of new technology requires a careful weighing among organizational needs, individual needs, technical factors, and human factors in order to make technology a resource to people rather than a hindrance.

The Golden Age of Learning

The real problem is not whether machines think but whether men do.
— B.F. Skinner, *Contingencies of Reinforcement*

It is quite possible that the golden age of learning has not yet arrived. As the above quote suggests, learning must continue to be considered a human activity. However, new technologies such as networked computers will offer human beings instance access to unprecedented levels of information. In his book *The Digital Economy*, Don Tapscott mentions "The Six Themes of the New Learning":

- ◆ **Theme 1:** Increasingly, work and learning are becoming the same thing
- ◆ **Theme 2:** Learning is becoming a lifelong challenge
- ◆ **Theme 3:** Learning is shifting away from the formal schools and universities
- ◆ **Theme 4:** Some educational institutions are working hard to reinvent themselves for relevance, but progress is slow
- ◆ **Theme 5:** Organizational consciousness is required to create learning organizations
- ◆ **Theme 6:** The new media can transform education, creating a working-learning infrastructure for the digital economy.

Themes 1, 2, and 6 are particularly relevant to this discussion. The learning profession must go beyond digitizing the same information that live instructors used to deliver. The learning technology revolution is not limited to making information available anytime, anywhere, in any amount, and at a lower cost. The learning technology revolution can enable a new process for learning that is more enjoyable, more self-directed, more immersive, and results in much higher retention rates than the current educational process. This new process of learning will model the Socratic process of education through inquiry. Learning technologies can allow learners to participate in the design of their own curriculum while being guided by online mentors who propose important questions about their choices. As Tapscott commented, it is now possible to "customize down to the individual." Learning professionals can innovate new ways of making formal education seem informal. While pioneers such as Malcolm Knowles have paved the way toward self-directed learning, it is now possible to go further into a more immersive self-discovery of knowledge.

The ultimate goal will be to make the process of self-discovery more efficient and practical. Although experience is the best teacher, it is also a notoriously slow and expensive learning process. Through technology, new systems can be created for accelerating experiential learning.

This study has started an important discussion of what the technological revolution has to offer to the field of learning. It has also examined the skills and knowledge practitioners need to select, manage, and use the technologies themselves. Future studies will need to examine how technology will change the process of learning for the learner and what competencies the learners will need to learn via technology. In other words, future studies will need to look at this same topic from the learner's perspective rather than the practitioner's perspective. As Dr. William J. Rothwell puts it, studying the competencies for practitioners is "a bit like studying the birthing process from the father's perspective."

It's Not Education at a Distance

In the project framework, it was mentioned that ASTD chose not to include the term "distance learning" in the list of learning technologies. While one reason for this is the ambiguous definition of this term, another important reason is that it connotes distance rather than closeness. Just as AT&T markets the telephone as a way to "reach out and touch someone," digital training materials must reside within the learner's world, and the learner must always feel that help is just around the corner. This will be more than a technical challenge. Instructional designers will need to innovate ways of becoming part of the learner's world without ever meeting or even speaking with the learner in person. In effect, the future world of learning will need to become as "real" and as intimate for learners as TV characters have been for the past four decades.

It is also important to resist the idea that learning technologies are a lesser alternative to classroom learning. Although there isn't clear proof that learning via technology provides a richer experience for the learner, there isn't any indication that it is a lesser experience either. Initial studies have shown that learning via technology is at least equal to the classroom experience. The quality of the instructional design is much more important than the method in which it is delivered. The future of learning technologies, therefore, does not reside in how advanced the technologies become, but rather in how well we employ these technologies for learning purposes.

SECTION 8   Assessment Tools
By Ethan S. Sanders

We hope that the preceding pages have given you a better understanding of the competencies for learning technologies and their application in the world of training and development. In order to help you apply this new knowledge to your own circumstances, we have developed several assessment tools. This section includes the following inventories:

Worksheet 1: Self-Assessment Inventory

Worksheet 2: Assessment Inventory

Worksheet 3: Summary of Results

Worksheet 4: Development Planning Tool

Worksheet 5: Learning Contract

These inventories can be used to gather a 360-degree assessment of your strengths and development needs in relation to the use, selection, and management of learning technologies. They also help you to understand which competencies are important to develop for your current work situation and which competencies will become increasingly important in the future. Once you have this information, worksheet 4 will help you to brainstorm ways of filling your knowledge gaps, and worksheet 5 will help you to formalize your development objectives into a learning contract.

By following the directions at the top of each worksheet, you can complete this process in a few hours.

Section A: Purpose of this self-assessment.

Which of the following reasons best describes your purpose for wanting to complete a competency review process? Answering this question is important because your reason(s) will affect what you need from the competency assessment process and how you should interpret the results. Place a check in all of the appropriate boxes below. You may want to rank your answers, starting with "1" as your primary reason, "2" as your secondary reason, and so on.

- ❏ To benchmark myself against the competencies described in this book.

- ❏ To move into a new role within a training department that involves a great amount of responsibility for using, selecting, or managing learning technologies.

- ❏ To document my current competency level with learning technologies.

- ❏ To determine how technology will change my current job in the foreseeable future.

- ❏ To benchmark my current skills against other training professionals.

- ❏ To use as a supplement to my performance review.

- ❏ Other: _____

Section B: Identifying reviewers.

Given your reason(s) for entering this review process, consider which individuals within your organization would best be able to assess your present competency level objectively. It is also possible to select people who are not within your organization, but they must be familiar with your work. It is important that you select several (two or three) of your peers, and if you manage people, several of your direct reports. If you do not have any direct reports, consider people in other departments who you interact with daily. Also, in order to gain a well-rounded perspective, you need to involve your direct supervisor in this process. Please list all of your potential candidates in the spaces provided on the following pages.

Worksheet 1: Self-Assessment Inventory

Peers:

1. Name: _____

   Job Title and Work Function: _____

   _____

   _____

   _____

   Why will this person provide helpful information? _____

   _____

   _____

   _____

2. Name: _____

   Job Title and Work Function: _____

   _____

   _____

   _____

   Why will this person provide helpful information? _____

   _____

   _____

   _____

3. Name: _____

   Job Title and Work Function: _____

   _____

   _____

   _____

   Why will this person provide helpful information? _____

   _____

   _____

   _____

This worksheet is reproducible.

Direct Reports:

1. Name: _____

    Job Title and Work Function: _____

    _____

    _____

    _____

    Why will this person provide helpful information? _____

    _____

    _____

    _____

2. Name: _____

    Job Title and Work Function: _____

    _____

    _____

    _____

    Why will this person provide helpful information? _____

    _____

    _____

    _____

3. Name: _____

    Job Title and Work Function: _____

    _____

    _____

    _____

    Why will this person provide helpful information? _____

    _____

    _____

    _____

This worksheet is reproducible.

Supervisor:

1. Name: _____

    Job Title and Work Function: _____

    _____

    _____

    _____

    Why will this person provide helpful information? _____

    _____

    _____

    _____

2. Name: _____

    Job Title and Work Function: _____

    _____

    _____

    _____

    Why will this person provide helpful information? _____

    _____

    _____

    _____

3. Name: _____

    Job Title and Work Function: _____

    _____

    _____

    _____

    Why will this person provide helpful information? _____

    _____

    _____

    _____

This worksheet is reproducible.

Section C: Rate yourself

1. Rate your expertise in each competency area by circling the appropriate number under "Current Level of Expertise." Use the following definitions to help you identify your level of expertise:

- None (0): I have very little knowledge of, or experience in, applying this competency to learning technologies.

- Basic (1-2): I possess general understanding of key principles, and I am capable of making simple decisions regarding the proper application of this competency to learning technologies.

- Intermediate (3-4): I possess a comprehensive understanding of key principles, and I am capable of making complex decisions regarding the application of this competency to learning technologies.

- Advanced (5-6): I possess substantial knowledge and expertise and can work in complex situations that require the application of this competency to learning technologies.

Use the higher number if you feel strongly that you have reached this level of expertise. Use the lower number if you are less confident that you have reached this level.

2. Cover up your "Current Level of Expertise" answers. Go to the last column on the right and rate on a scale from 1 to 4 how important you think this competency is for your future success in the field of learning technologies. This assessment should be completely independent of which competencies you think you already have or don't have. Here is what the numbers correspond to:

- 1: not important to future success

- 2: somewhat important to future success

- 3: important to future success

- 4: very important to future success

Worksheet 1: Self-Assessment Inventory

General Competencies	Current Level of Expertise							Future Importance			
	None	Basic		Intermediate		Advanced		How important is this competency for future success?			
1. **Adult Learning:** Understanding how adults learn and how they use knowledge, skills, and attitudes.	0	1	2	3	4	5	6	1	2	3	4
2. **Instructional Design:** Using the ISD model (analysis, design, development, delivery, evaluation) for creating adult education classes that fulfill organizational goals.	0	1	2	3	4	5	6	1	2	3	4
3. **Performance Gap Analysis:** Performing "front-end analysis" by comparing actual and ideal performance levels in the workplace. Identifying opportunities and strategies for improving performance.	0	1	2	3	4	5	6	1	2	3	4
4. **Change Management:** Helping people adapt to the changes brought on by new technologies and helping them to see the value and benefits of new technologies.	0	1	2	3	4	5	6	1	2	3	4
5. **Leadership:** Leading, influencing, and coaching others to help them achieve desired results.	0	1	2	3	4	5	6	1	2	3	4
6. **Industry Awareness:** Understanding the current and future climate of one's company's industry and formulating strategies that respond to that climate.	0	1	2	3	4	5	6	1	2	3	4
7. **Buy-in/Advocacy:** Building ownership and support for workplace initiatives.	0	1	2	3	4	5	6	1	2	3	4

This worksheet is reproducible.

Worksheet 1: Self-Assessment Inventory (continued)

General Competencies	Current Level of Expertise							Future Importance			
	None	Basic		Intermediate		Advanced		How important is this competency for future success?			
	0	1	2	3	4	5	6	1	2	3	4
8. Interpersonal Relationship Building/Collaboration: Effectively interacting with others in order to produce meaningful outcomes.	0	1	2	3	4	5	6	1	2	3	4
9. Consulting: Helping clients and stakeholders to question their assumptions, determine their needs, and plan implementation strategies for achieving their goals.	0	1	2	3	4	5	6	1	2	3	4
10. Business Knowledge: Demonstrating awareness of business functions and how business decisions affect financial and nonfinancial work results.	0	1	2	3	4	5	6	1	2	3	4
11. Systems Thinking: Recognizing the interrelationship among the driving forces that connect seemingly isolated incidents within the organization. Also taking a holistic view of performance problems in order to find the root causes.	0	1	2	3	4	5	6	1	2	3	4
12. Contracting: Negotiating, organizing, preparing, monitoring, and evaluating work performed by vendors and consultants.	0	1	2	3	4	5	6	1	2	3	4
13. Project Management: Assessing, planning, negotiating, organizing, monitoring, and evaluating the delivery process. Effectively managing human, capital, and financial resources.	0	1	2	3	4	5	6	1	2	3	4
14. Awareness of Learning Technology Industry: Having a general understanding of trends within the learning technology industry and knowing the existing and emerging technologies.	0	1	2	3	4	5	6	1	2	3	4
15. Communication: Applying effective verbal, nonverbal, and written communication methods to achieve desired results.	0	1	2	3	4	5	6	1	2	3	4

This worksheet is reproducible.

General Competencies	Current Level of Expertise							Future Importance			
	None	Basic		Intermediate		Advanced		How important is this competency for future success?			
	0	1	2	3	4	5	6	1	2	3	4
16. Program Evaluation: Measuring the success of learning interventions.	0	1	2	3	4	5	6	1	2	3	4
17. Design and Development: Deciding which combination of instructional methods, presentation methods, and distribution methods will best deliver the final program to the learner. Outlining and creating instructional materials that are suitable for electronic dissemination.	0	1	2	3	4	5	6	1	2	3	4
18. Implementation and Support: Coordinating the installation and maintenance of learning technologies.	0	1	2	3	4	5	6	1	2	3	4

This worksheet is reproducible.

Management Competencies	Current Level of Expertise							Future Importance			
	None	Basic		Intermediate		Advanced		How important is this competency for future success?			
	0	1	2	3	4	5	6	1	2	3	4
19. **Management of Learning Technology Selection:** Supervising the selection of learning technologies and assuring that these selections meet organizational needs. Determining when, how, and where learning technologies should be used and monitoring the progress of all the other roles in the delivery process.	0	1	2	3	4	5	6	1	2	3	4
20. **Management of Learning Technology Design and Development:** Supervising and assuring the effective integration of performance objectives, course materials, and learning technologies into a design document that fulfills the organization's goals.	0	1	2	3	4	5	6	1	2	3	4
21. **Management of Learning Technology Implementation, Support, and Evaluation:** Supervising the installation and maintenance of learning technologies and assuring that all systems continuously meet company specifications.	0	1	2	3	4	5	6	1	2	3	4

This worksheet is reproducible.

Distribution Method Competencies	Current Level of Expertise							Future Importance			
	None	Basic		Intermediate		Advanced		How important is this competency for future success?			
22. Cost Analysis/ROI of the Distribution Methods: Understanding the relative costs of each distribution method, or combination of methods, and assuring that the organization is receiving a good value for the dollars spent on these technologies.	0	1	2	3	4	5	6	1	2	3	4
23. Limitations and Benefits of the Distribution Methods: Knowing the true capabilities of each distribution method, or combination of methods, and tying these capabilities in with the needs of the organization.	0	1	2	3	4	5	6	1	2	3	4
24. Effect of Distribution Method on Learners: Assessing how various distribution methods, or combination of methods, will cater to individual learning styles. Balancing learner needs against organizational needs.	0	1	2	3	4	5	6	1	2	3	4
25. Integration of Distribution Methods: Mixing distribution methods in an effective and efficient manner to facilitate learning.	0	1	2	3	4	5	6	1	2	3	4
26. Remote Site Coordination: Coordinating the installation and maintenance of distribution technologies at a remote site and assuring that all systems continuously meet design specifications.	0	1	2	3	4	5	6	1	2	3	4
27. Technology Evaluation: Assuring that all component technologies continuously meet technical design and performance specifications.	0	1	2	3	4	5	6	1	2	3	4

This worksheet is reproducible.

Worksheet 1: Self-Assessment Inventory (continued)

Presentation Method Competencies	Current Level of Expertise							Future Importance
	None	Basic		Intermediate		Advanced		How important is this competency for future success?
28. **Cost Analysis/ROI of the Presentation Methods:** Understanding the relative costs of each presentation method, or combination of methods, and assuring that the organization is receiving a good value for the dollars spent on these technologies.	0	1	2	3	4	5	6	1 2 3 4
29. **Limitations and Benefits of the Presentation Methods:** Knowing the true capabilities of each presentation method, or combination of methods, and tying these capabilities in with the needs of the organization.	0	1	2	3	4	5	6	1 2 3 4
30. **Effect of Presentation Method on Learners:** Assessing how various presentation methods, or combination of methods, will cater to individual learning styles. Balancing learner needs against organizational needs.	0	1	2	3	4	5	6	1 2 3 4
31. **Integration of Presentation Methods:** Mixing presentation methods in an effective and efficient manner to facilitate learning.	0	1	2	3	4	5	6	1 2 3 4

This worksheet is reproducible.

Worksheet 2: Assessment Inventory

On the following pages, you will find the assessment inventory that your peers, direct reports, and supervisor will use. At the top of the worksheet, respondents are given an opportunity to identify themselves and to state their relationship to you. Although this information is helpful, the respondents should be allowed to turn in the inventory anonymously. Only your supervisor must reveal his or her identity. We have also supplied you with a cover page that you can use when distributing the inventory. Here are some steps and important guidelines to remember:

Guidelines:

1. Ask people if they are interested in participating in this activity before you send them the inventory.

2. Tell them clearly what this inventory is being used for, how long it will take, and when it is due.

3. Advise respondents that they may turn in this inventory anonymously if they so choose. Let your supervisor know that his or her responses cannot be given anonymously.

4. Tell respondents that you want candid, future-focused feedback, but not a personality or performance appraisal. Make them comfortable with the idea of providing honest feedback. Tell them that after you've reviewed the completed assessment, you may come back to clarify, but not challenge, their responses (if they chose to put their name on the inventory).

Steps:

1. Make photocopies of the Assessment Inventory. You will need one copy for each respondent who you intend to have complete it.

2. Make photocopies of the cover sheet, which is on the next page. Be sure to address a cover sheet to each respondent, fill out the necessary information, and staple it to the front of the inventory.

3. Distribute the inventory to the respondents.

4. Send out a reminder notice a few days before the inventory is due.

5. Collect the inventories on the due date, and complete worksheet 3 "Summary of Results."

Cover Sheet for Assessment Inventory

From: _____ To: _____ Date:_____

Thank you for agreeing to participate in this competency assessment activity. I am trying to determine which competencies are strengths for me and which competencies I need to develop. Please give me candid, future-focused, and honest feedback of my competencies. Below is a full set of instructions. If you need any further clarification, feel free to call me at (_____) _____. The competencies that you are measuring me against were derived from the *ASTD Models for Learning Technologies*. They describe the major competencies that are necessary to select, manage, and use learning technologies. If you have any difficulty understanding what these competencies are referring to, please call me for more information. Again, thank you for participating in this activity. The due date is _____.

Directions: Please think about the person who has asked you to complete this assessment. You can help this person by giving him or her feedback based on your personal observations of his or her work. Although this questionnaire is not a performance appraisal, answering the following questions will provide helpful guidance for this person to develop into expanded roles within the organization. Here are the steps you need to follow:

1. Indicate in the first column if you have observed the person demonstrating the competency that is described. If you have not observed the person demonstrating this competency, skip to the next competency. If you have observed the person demonstrating this competency, go to step #2.

2. On a scale from 0 to 6, give the person an idea of how proficient he or she is in this competency. Use the following definitions to help you identify the person's level of expertise:

◆ None (0): Possesses very little knowledge of, or experience in, applying this competency to learning technologies.
◆ Basic (1-2): Possesses general understanding of key principles and is capable of making simple decisions regarding the proper application of this competency to learning technologies.
◆ Intermediate (3-4): Possesses a comprehensive understanding of key principles and is capable of making complex decisions regarding the application of this competency to learning technologies.
◆ Advanced (5-6): Possesses substantial knowledge and expertise and can work in complex situations that require the application of this competency to learning technologies.

Use the higher number if you feel strongly that the person has reached this level of expertise. Use the lower number if you are less confident that he or she has reached this

level. You will need the following definitions to help you in this assessment:

Learning Technologies: Electronic technologies that deliver information and facilitate the development of skills and knowledge.
Presentation Methods: The manner in which information is presented to learners (for example, electronic text, multimedia, virtual reality, audio, and so on).
Distribution Methods: The manner in which information is delivered to learners (for example, satellite, cable TV, the Web, computer disks, and so on).

3. Finally, cover up the "Current Level of Expertise" answers. Go to the last column on the right and rate on a scale from 1 to 4 how important you think this competency is for the person's future success in the field of learning technologies. **Remember, this assessment should be completely independent of which competencies you think the person being rated already has or does not have.** Here is what the numbers correspond to:

◆ 1: not important to future success
◆ 2: somewhat important to future success
◆ 3: important to future success
◆ 4: very important to future success

Example:

Worksheet 2: Assessment Inventory

General Competencies	Have they demonstrated this competency?	Current Level of Expertise							Future Importance How important is this competency for future success?
		None	Basic		Intermediate		Advanced		
		0	1	2	3	4	5	6	1 2 3 4
1. Adult Learning: Understanding how adults learn and how they use knowledge, skills, and attitudes.	☑ Yes ☐ No	0	1	2	3	④	5	6	1 2 ③ 4

Name of Person Being Reviewed: _____ Date: _____

Reviewer's Name (optional): _____

Relationship: The Person Being Reviewed is My:　❑ Direct Report　　❑ Peer　　❑ Supervisor

Worksheet 2: Assessment Inventory

General Competencies	Have they demonstrated this competency?	Current Level of Expertise							Future Importance
		None	Basic		Intermediate		Advanced		How important is this competency for future success?
1. Adult Learning: Understanding how adults learn and how they use knowledge, skills, and attitudes.	❑ **Yes** ❑ **No**	0	1	2	3	4	5	6	1　2　3　4
2. Instructional Design: Using the ISD model (analysis, design, development, delivery, evaluation) for creating adult education classes that fulfill organizational goals.	❑ **Yes** ❑ **No**	0	1	2	3	4	5	6	1　2　3　4
3. Performance Gap Analysis: Performing "front-end analysis" by comparing actual and ideal performance levels in the workplace. Identifying opportunities and strategies for improving performance.	❑ **Yes** ❑ **No**	0	1	2	3	4	5	6	1　2　3　4
4. Change Management: Helping people adapt to the changes brought on by new technologies and helping them to see the value and benefits of new technologies.	❑ **Yes** ❑ **No**	0	1	2	3	4	5	6	1　2　3　4
5. Leadership: Leading, influencing, and coaching others to help them achieve desired results.	❑ **Yes** ❑ **No**	0	1	2	3	4	5	6	1　2　3　4
6. Industry Awareness: Understanding the current and future climate of one's company's industry and formulating strategies that respond to that climate.	❑ **Yes** ❑ **No**	0	1	2	3	4	5	6	1　2　3　4
7. Buy-in/Advocacy: Building ownership and support for workplace initiatives.	❑ **Yes** ❑ **No**	0	1	2	3	4	5	6	1　2　3　4

This worksheet is reproducible.

General Competencies	Have they demonstrated this competency?	Current Level of Expertise							Future Importance
		None	Basic		Intermediate		Advanced		How important is this competency for future success?
8. Interpersonal Relationship Building/Collaboration: Effectively interacting with others in order to produce meaningful outcomes.	❏ **Yes** ❏ **No**	0	1	2	3	4	5	6	1 2 3 4
9. Consulting: Helping clients and stakeholders to question their assumptions, determine their needs, and plan implementation strategies for achieving their goals.	❏ **Yes** ❏ **No**	0	1	2	3	4	5	6	1 2 3 4
10. Business Knowledge: Demonstrating awareness of business functions and how business decisions affect financial and nonfinancial work results.	❏ **Yes** ❏ **No**	0	1	2	3	4	5	6	1 2 3 4
11. Systems Thinking: Recognizing the interrelationship among the driving forces that connect seemingly isolated incidents within the organization. Also taking a holistic view of performance problems in order to find the root causes.	❏ **Yes** ❏ **No**	0	1	2	3	4	5	6	1 2 3 4
12. Contracting: Negotiating, organizing, preparing, monitoring, and evaluating work performed by vendors and consultants.	❏ **Yes** ❏ **No**	0	1	2	3	4	5	6	1 2 3 4
13. Project Management: Assessing, planning, negotiating, organizing, monitoring, and evaluating the delivery process. Effectively managing human, capital, and financial resources.	❏ **Yes** ❏ **No**	0	1	2	3	4	5	6	1 2 3 4
14. Awareness of Learning Technology Industry: Having a general understanding of trends within the learning technology industry and knowing the existing and emerging technologies.	❏ **Yes** ❏ **No**	0	1	2	3	4	5	6	1 2 3 4
15. Communication: Applying effective verbal, nonverbal, and written communication methods to achieve desired results.	❏ **Yes** ❏ **No**	0	1	2	3	4	5	6	1 2 3 4

This worksheet is reproducible.

General Competencies	Have they demonstrated this competency?	Current Level of Expertise							Future Importance
		None	Basic		Intermediate		Advanced		How important is this competency for future success?
16. Program Evaluation: Measuring the success of learning interventions.	❑ **Yes** ❑ **No**	0	1	2	3	4	5	6	1 2 3 4
17. Design and Development: Deciding which combination of instructional methods, presentation methods, and distribution methods will best deliver the final program to the learner. Outlining and creating instructional materials that are suitable for electronic dissemination.	❑ **Yes** ❑ **No**	0	1	2	3	4	5	6	1 2 3 4
18. Implementation and Support: Coordinating the installation and maintenance of learning technologies.	❑ **Yes** ❑ **No**	0	1	2	3	4	5	6	1 2 3 4

This worksheet is reproducible.

Worksheet 2: Assessment Inventory (continued)

Management Competencies	Have they demonstrated this competency?	Current Level of Expertise							Future Importance
		None	Basic		Intermediate		Advanced		How important is this competency for future success?
19. Management of Learning Technology Selection: Supervising the selection of learning technologies and assuring that these selections meet organizational needs. Determining when, how, and where learning technologies should be used and monitoring the progress of all the other roles in the delivery process.	❏ **Yes** ❏ **No**	0	1	2	3	4	5	6	1 2 3 4
20. Management of Learning Technology Design and Development: Supervising and assuring the effective integration of performance objectives, course materials, and learning technologies into a design document that fulfills the organization's goals.	❏ **Yes** ❏ **No**	0	1	2	3	4	5	6	1 2 3 4
21. Management of Learning Technology Implementation, Support, and Evaluation: Supervising the installation and maintenance of learning technologies and assuring that all systems continuously meet company specifications.	❏ **Yes** ❏ **No**	0	1	2	3	4	5	6	1 2 3 4

This worksheet is reproducible.

Distribution Method Competencies	Have they demonstrated this competency?	Current Level of Expertise							Future Importance
		None	Basic		Intermediate		Advanced		How important is this competency for future success?
		0	1	2	3	4	5	6	1 2 3 4
22. Cost Analysis/ROI of the Distribution Methods: Understanding the relative costs of each distribution method, or combination of methods, and assuring that the organization is receiving a good value for the dollars spent on these technologies.	❑ **Yes** ❑ **No**	0	1	2	3	4	5	6	1 2 3 4
23. Limitations and Benefits of the Distribution Methods: Knowing the true capabilities of each distribution method, or combination of methods, and tying these capabilities in with the needs of the organization.	❑ **Yes** ❑ **No**	0	1	2	3	4	5	6	1 2 3 4
24. Effect of Distribution Method on Learners: Assessing how various distribution methods, or combination of methods, will cater to individual learning styles. Balancing learner needs against organizational needs.	❑ **Yes** ❑ **No**	0	1	2	3	4	5	6	1 2 3 4
25. Integration of Distribution Methods: Mixing distribution methods in an effective and efficient manner to facilitate learning.	❑ **Yes** ❑ **No**	0	1	2	3	4	5	6	1 2 3 4
26. Remote Site Coordination: Coordinating the installation and maintenance of distribution technologies at a remote site and assuring that all systems continuously meet design specifications.	❑ **Yes** ❑ **No**	0	1	2	3	4	5	6	1 2 3 4
27. Technology Evaluation: Assuring that all component technologies continuously meet technical design and performance specifications.	❑ **Yes** ❑ **No**	0	1	2	3	4	5	6	1 2 3 4

This worksheet is reproducible.

Presentation Method Competencies	Have they demonstrated this competency?	Current Level of Expertise							Future Importance
		None	Basic		Intermediate		Advanced		How important is this competency for future success?
28. **Cost Analysis/ROI of the Presentation Methods:** Understanding the relative costs of each presentation method, or combination of methods, and assuring that the organization is receiving a good value for the dollars spent on these technologies.	❏ **Yes** ❏ **No**	0	1	2	3	4	5	6	1 2 3 4
29. **Limitations and Benefits of the Presentation Methods:** Knowing the true capabilities of each presentation method, or combination of methods, and tying these capabilities in with the needs of the organization.	❏ **Yes** ❏ **No**	0	1	2	3	4	5	6	1 2 3 4
30. **Effect of Presentation Method on Learners:** Assessing how various presentation methods, or combination of methods, will cater to individual learning styles. Balancing learner needs against organizational needs.	❏ **Yes** ❏ **No**	0	1	2	3	4	5	6	1 2 3 4
31. **Integration of Presentation Methods:** Mixing presentation methods in an effective and efficient manner to facilitate learning.	❏ **Yes** ❏ **No**	0	1	2	3	4	5	6	1 2 3 4

This worksheet is reproducible.

Section A:

Use the worksheet below to summarize and analyze the results of your data collection. Here are the steps you want to follow:

1. Each competency below has two rows for entering data. In the top row, enter the assessment scores that you received for your current level of expertise. (1–6) In the bottom row, enter the assessment scores for the future importance of the competency. (1–4)

2. For each "current level" row, write in all of the scores that you received from your direct reports in the cell provided. Do the same for your self-assessment scores, all of your peers' scores, and your supervisor's score. If a respondent checked "no" in the second column for a competency in the Assessment Inventory, do not include a score for that item, and divide the total score by one less response.

3. Add all the scores together, and write the total in the appropriate cell.

4. Divide the sum total by the number of responses that you received. Write the average in the appropriate cell.

5. Repeat the above steps for the "future importance" scores for each competency.

Example:

Worksheet 3: Summary of Results

General Competencies		Direct Reports	Self	Peers	Supervisor	Totals	Averages
1. Adult Learning: Understanding how adults learn and how they use knowledge, skills, and attitudes.	Current	5, 6, 3	2	4, 5, 5	6	36	4.5
	Future	4, 3, 4	3	4, 4, 5	2	29	3.63

General Competencies		Direct Reports	Self	Peers	Supervisor	Totals	Averages
1. Adult Learning: Understanding how adults learn and how they use knowledge, skills, and attitudes.	Current						
	Future						
2. Instructional Design: Using the ISD model (analysis, design, development, delivery, evaluation) for creating adult education classes that fulfill organizational goals.	Current						
	Future						
3. Performance Gap Analysis: Performing "front-end analysis" by comparing actual and ideal performance levels in the workplace. Identifying opportunities and strategies for improving performance.	Current						
	Future						
4. Change Management: Helping people adapt to the changes brought on by new technologies and helping them to see the value and benefits of new technologies.	Current						
	Future						
5. Leadership: Leading, influencing, and coaching others to help them achieve desired results.	Current						
	Future						
6. Industry Awareness: Understanding the current and future climate of one's company's industry and formulating strategies that respond to that climate.	Current						
	Future						
7. Buy-in/Advocacy: Building ownership and support for workplace initiatives.	Current						
	Future						

This worksheet is reproducible.

General Competencies		Direct Reports	Self	Peers	Supervisor	Totals
8. Interpersonal Relationship Building/Collaboration: Effectively interacting with others in order to produce meaningful outcomes.	Current					
	Future					
9. Consulting: Helping clients and stakeholders to question their assumptions, determine their needs, and plan implementation strategies for achieving their goals.	Current					
	Future					
10. Business Knowledge: Demonstrating awareness of business functions and how business decisions affect financial and nonfinancial work results.	Current					
	Future					
11. Systems Thinking: Recognizing the interrelationship among the driving forces that connect seemingly isolated incidents within the organization. Also taking a holistic view of performance problems in order to find the root causes.	Current					
	Future					
12. Contracting: Negotiating, organizing, preparing, monitoring, and evaluating work performed by vendors and consultants.	Current					
	Future					
13. Project Management: Assessing, planning, negotiating, organizing, monitoring, and evaluating the delivery process. Effectively managing human, capital, and financial resources.	Current					
	Future					
14. Awareness of Learning Technology Industry: Having a general understanding of trends within the learning technology industry and knowing the existing and emerging technologies.	Current					
	Future					
15. Communication: Applying effective verbal, nonverbal, and written communication methods to achieve desired results.	Current					
	Future					

This worksheet is reproducible.

General Competencies		Direct Reports	Self	Peers	Supervisor	Totals	Averages
16. Program Evaluation: Measuring the success of learning interventions.	Current						
	Future						
17. Design and Development: Deciding which combination of instructional methods, presentation methods, and distribution methods will best deliver the final program to the learner. Outlining and creating instructional materials that are suitable for electronic dissemination.	Current						
	Future						
18. Implementation and Support: Coordinating the installation and maintenance of learning technologies.	Current						
	Future						

This worksheet is reproducible.

Management Competencies		Direct Reports	Self	Peers	Supervisor	Totals	Averages
19. Management of Learning Technology Selection: Supervising the selection of learning technologies and assuring that these selections meet organizational needs. Determining when, how, and where learning technologies should be used and monitoring the progress of all the other roles in the delivery process.	Current						
	Future						
20. Management of Learning Technology Design and Development: Supervising and assuring the effective integration of performance objectives, course materials, and learning technologies into a design document that fulfills the organization's goals.	Current						
	Future						
21. Management of Learning Technology Implementation, Support, and Evaluation: Supervising the installation and maintenance of learning technologies and assuring that all systems continuously meet company specifications.	Current						
	Future						

This worksheet is reproducible.

Distribution Method Competencies		Direct Reports	Self	Peers	Supervisor	Totals	Averages
22. Cost Analysis/ROI of the Distribution Methods: Understanding the relative costs of each distribution method, or combination of methods, and assuring that the organization is receiving a good value for the dollars spent on these technologies.	Current						
	Future						
23. Limitations and Benefits of the Distribution Methods: Knowing the true capabilities of each distribution method, or combination of methods, and tying these capabilities in with the needs of the organization.	Current						
	Future						
24. Effect of Distribution Method on Learners: Assessing how various distribution methods, or combination of methods, will cater to individual learning styles. Balancing learner needs against organizational needs.	Current						
	Future						
25. Integration of Distribution Methods: Mixing distribution methods in an effective and efficient manner to facilitate learning.	Current						
	Future						
26. Remote Site Coordination: Coordinating the installation and maintenance of distribution technologies at a remote site and assuring that all systems continuously meet design specifications.	Current						
	Future						
27. Technology Evaluation: Assuring that all component technologies continuously meet technical design and performance specifications.	Current						
	Future						

This worksheet is reproducible.

Presentation Method Competencies		Direct Reports	Self	Peers	Supervisor	Totals	Averages
28. Cost Analysis/ROI of the Presentation Methods: Understanding the relative costs of each presentation method, or combination of methods, and assuring that the organization is receiving a good value for the dollars spent on these technologies.	Current						
	Future						
29. Limitations and Benefits of the Presentation Methods: Knowing the true capabilities of each presentation method, or combination of methods, and tying these capabilities in with the needs of the organization.	Current						
	Future						
30. Effect of Presentation Method on Learners: Assessing how various presentation methods, or combination of methods, will cater to individual learning styles. Balancing learner needs against organizational needs.	Current						
	Future						
31. Integration of Presentation Methods: Mixing presentation methods in an effective and efficient manner to facilitate learning.	Current						
	Future						

This worksheet is reproducible.

Section B:

1. Based on the current and future average scores from section A in this worksheet, plot each competency's position on the graph supplied below. Draw a dot and the number of the competency in the appropriate place on the chart. For example, if "adult learning" had an average current score of "5.8" and an average future score of "1.43" it would appear as shown below.

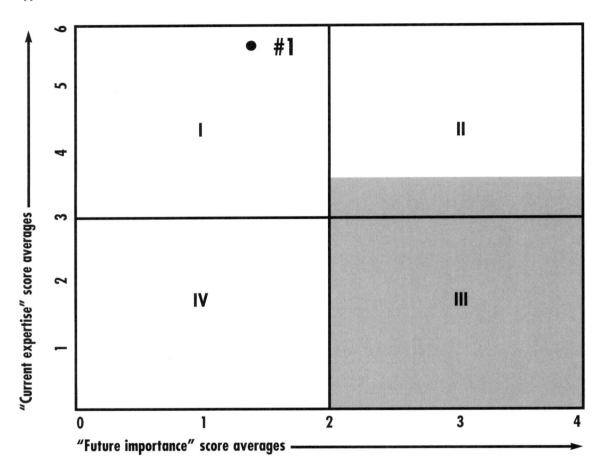

Once you have plotted all 31 competencies, take a long look at the chart. The competencies that fall within the shaded area are the ones that the average respondent thought to be very important to future success in the field. These are also the competencies that require the greatest amount of development. In particular, the closer the competency is to the lower, right corner of the graph, the more immediate the developmental need.

This worksheet is reproducible.

2. Based on the information from above, list some ideas that you have for developing the competencies that fall within the shaded area:

_____

_____

_____

_____

3. Go back and compare your self-assessment score for each competency to the average score. Write down all of the competencies below where your self-assessment score is more than two points higher or lower than the average. Next to each competency, write down some reasons why your self-assessment was so much different than the average assessment.

Competency Name: _____   Reason for difference: _____

Competency Name: _____   Reason for difference: _____

Competency Name: _____   Reason for difference: _____

Competency Name: _____   Reason for difference: _____

Competency Name: _____   Reason for difference: _____

Competency Name: _____   Reason for difference: _____

4. Consider all of the information above, and then create a list of objectives that would move you toward greater expertise in important competency areas. Use more paper if necessary.

Objective #1: _____

Objective #2: _____

Objective #3: _____

Objective #4: _____

This worksheet is reproducible.

Worksheet 4: Development Planning Tool

There are many ways to build new competencies, and many resources are available to help in that process. The following is a brief review of some possible ways:

- Talk to other people.
- Work with other people on short-term or long-term projects.
- Observe and imitate role models.
- Participate in formal or informal learning groups.
- Attend college courses.
- Participate in online courses.
- Search the Internet on topics that are related to learning technologies.
- Attend nondegree continuing education seminars.
- Participate in professional associations.
- Use networks (online or interpersonal).
- Read periodicals, journals, or newsletters.
- Read books.
- Watch videotapes.
- Listen to audiocassettes.
- Use software or multimedia-based learning methods.
- Attend conferences.

Use the following worksheet to generate ideas on how to develop the competencies that are necessary for success in the field of learning technologies. Here are the steps you should follow:

1. List a competency that you need to develop and consider how to use the suggestions listed in the left column.

2. Make notes in the right column about ways to implement the suggestions in order to build proficiency.

3. Remember that there are not any "right" or "wrong" answers.

4. Add more paper if needed.

Example:

Competency Name: _____*Adult Learning*_____

Example:

Ways to Build the Competency	Ideas on How to Implement Suggestions
• *Talk to other people.*	• *Get Joe's suggestions on how to build this competency.* • *Ask Mary about that course she took on adult learning.* • *Call ASTD and see if they will give me an information interview over the phone.*

Worksheet 4: Development Planning Tool (continued)

Competency Name: _____

Ways to Build the Competency	Ideas on How to Implement Suggestions
• Talk to other people.	• • •
• Work with other people on short-term or long-term projects.	• • •
• Observe and imitate role models.	• • •
• Participate in formal or informal learning groups.	• • •
• Attend college courses.	• • •
• Participate in online courses.	• • •
• Search the Internet on topics that are related to learning technologies.	• • •
• Attend nondegree continuing education seminars.	• • •
• Participate in professional associations.	• • •
• Use networks (online or interpersonal).	• • •
• Read periodicals, journals, or newsletters.	• • •
• Read books.	• • •
• Watch videotapes.	• • •
• Listen to audiocassettes.	• • •
• Use software or multimedia-based learning methods.	• • •
• Attend conferences.	• • •

This worksheet is reproducible.

Worksheet 5: Learning Contract

The idea behind a learning contract is to formalize your objectives into a plan of action. This can be a very valuable tool for gaining the support of your supervisor, your co-workers, and your organization. It also will help you to track your progress towards your goals. To complete this learning contract, follow these steps:

1. Fill out your first objective (transfer your objectives from worksheet 3, section B, question #4) for bridging the gaps between your current competencies and the competencies that you will need for future success. You will need a separate copy of the following worksheet for each objective that you state.

2. Fill in each activity that you believe will be needed in order to accomplish this objective.

3. Go back and estimate the amount of time each activity will take, the projected date for when it will be completed, what the deliverable will be (in other words, output), what evaluation criteria will be used to judge it, who will evaluate it, what resources will be needed, and what obstacles you may encounter.

4. When you have completed one worksheet for each objective, make an appointment to discuss it with your supervisor.

5. Negotiate the terms of the learning contract with your supervisor, update the learning contract, and get all parties involved to sign and date the document.

Example:

Objective #1 *To attain a higher level of competence in adult learning theory and application.*

Activities	Date/Number of Hours	Deliverable	Evaluation Criteria	Evaluator	Resources	Obstacles
Read Malcolm Knowles's book The Adult Learner: A Neglected Species and write a short paper.	*Finish by 12/15. 15 hours*	*2–3 page paper*	• *Clearly written.* • *Accurately describes the book.* • *Makes logical connection to my job.*	*My supervisor*	*The Adult Learner: A Neglected Species*	• *Not being able to make logical connections to my job.* • *Not finding enough time to read the book*

Employee's Signature: _____ Date: _____

Supervisor's Signature: _____ Date: _____

Worksheet 5: Learning Contract

Objective # _____ .

Activities	Date/Number of Hours	Deliverable	Evaluation Criteria	Evaluator	Resources	Obstacles

Employee's Signature: _____ Date: _____

Supervisor's Signature: _____ Date: _____

This worksheet is reproducible.

SECTION 9 RESOURCES AND REFERENCES
By Ethan S. Sanders

Info-lines

Here is a current list of *Info-line* publications on learning technologies:

- "Audio, Film, Video" (#8509)
- "Basics of Electronic Meeting Support" (#9507)
- "Basics of Electronic Performance Support Systems" (#9412)
- "The Basics of Internet Technology" (#9610)
- "Create Quality Videos" (#8607)
- "Delivering Quick-Response IBT/CBT Training" (#9701)
- "Effective Distance Learning" (#9607)

- "Ensure Learning from Training Films and Videos" (#8702)
- "Getting Inside Interactive Video" (#8510)
- "How to Build an Interface" (#9303)
- "How to Produce Quality Audio" (#9303)
- "Improve Training with Interactive Multimedia" (#9601)
- "Making EPSS Work for Your Organization" (#9501)
- "Write Successful Video Scripts" (#8707)

Web sites

Here is a list of Web sites to consider visiting as you do more research on this topic.

Web Site Name and Categories	URL (all begin with "http://")
Search Engines	
Excite	www.excite.com
Listserv Directory	www.liszt.com
Yahoo	www.yahoo.com
Alta Vista	altavista.digital.com
Lycos	www.lycos.com
Hotbot, The Wired Search Center	www.hotbot.com
Intranets	
The Complete Intranet Resource	www.intrack.com
Intranet Design Magazine	www.innergy.com
The Intranet Journal	www.intranetjournal.com
Intranet Partners	www.intranetpartners.com
Austin-Hayne Website	www.austin-hayne.com
LochNet USA	www.lochnet.com
David Strom's Web Informant	www.strom.com/pubwork/intra2.html
Research Sites	www.rhinrichs.com/library.htm#research
IntraNet Concepts	www.amdahl.com/doc/products/bsg/intra/concepts.html
Intranet Services	www.iserv.co.za/info.htm
The Intranet Journal	www.brill.com/intranet/ijx/index.html
Intranet World	www.internetnews.com/business/intranets.html
Computerworld Magazine	www.computerworld.com
CIO Magazine	www.cio.com
Netscape Intranet Whitepapers	home.netscape.com/comprod/at_work/white_paper/indepth.html#Apps

Web Site Name and Categories	URL (all begin with "http://")
Learning Theory and Assessment Tools	
The Institute for the Learning Sciences	www.ils.nwu.edu
ERIC Clearinghouse on Assessment & Evaluation	ericae2.educ.cua.edu
International Foundation for Action Learning	www.mentat.co.uk/park/ifal/
The International Management Centres	www.imc.org.uk/imc/
Performance Improvement	
EPSS.COM	www.epss.com
International Society for Performance Improvement	www.ispi.org
Technology	
CBT Solutions Magazine	www.cbtsolutions.com
EDUCOM	www.educom.edu
Frontiers in Education	fairway.ecn.purdue.edu/asee/fie95
Gil Gordon Associates	www.gilgordon.com
Presenters' University	presentersuniversity.com
Distance Learning	
Distance Education Clearinghouse	www.uwex.edu/disted/home.html
Center for Academic Computing	cac.psu.edu
Institute for Distance Education—Models of Distance Education	www.umuc.edu/ide/modlmenu.html
Howard University Distance Learning	www.con-ed.howard.edu
The Teletraining Institute	www.teletrain.com
U. of Wisconsin—Distance Learning Clearinghouse	www.uwex.edu/disted/home.html
Distance Education at a Glance	www.uidaho.edu/evo/distglan.html
Arizona State University—Distance Learning Technology	www-distlearn.pp.asu.edu
Priority Web Training E-mail Listserv	www.multimediatraining.com/training.html
Dyro's Web-Based Training Site	www.dyroweb.com
WBT Information Center	www.filename.com/wbt/index.html

Web Site Name and Categories	URL (all begin with "http://")
Web-Based Training	
WBT Information Center	www.filename.com/wbt/index.html
Dyro's Web-Based Training Site	www.dyroweb.com
Multimedia and Internet Training Newsletter	www.Multimediatraining.com/index.shtml
EPSS	
EPSS.COM	www.epss.com
The EPSS Info Site Home Page	www.tgx.com/enhance
EPSS Resources	itech1.coe.uga.edu/EPSS/EPSS.html
EPSS Info Site	www.tgx.com/enhance/dd_index.htm
Groupware	
Collaborative Strategies	www.collaborate.com
Lotus	www.lotus.com

Abrami, P.C. and Bures, E.M. (1996). Computer-supported collaborative learning and distance education. *American Journal of Distance Education, 10*(2), 37-42.

Adams, D.L. (1995). CD-I and training: A perfect fit? *Performance & Instruction, 34*(6), 28-33.

Adams, D.L. (1996). Another platform heard from. *Training & Development, 50*(5), 79-80.

Adams, D.L. (1996). Getting myself trained for Windows 95: Report cards on packaged courseware. *CBT Solutions,* July/Aug, 18-22.

Adams, N. (1995). Lessons from the virtual world. *Training, 32*(6), 45-48.

Allen, R.J. (1997). It's a circus out there. *CBT Solutions,* Mar/Apr, 1, 8-20.

Allen, R.J. and Chapman, B.L. (1996). What we learned in teaching teachers to teach. *CBT Solutions,* Sep/Oct, 14-24.

Anderson, S. and Gibson, M. (1994). Managing CBI projects. *Journal of Interactive Instruction Development, 6*(3), 32-37.

Anfuso, D. (1995). Colgate's global HR unites under one strategy. *Personnel Journal, 74*(10), 44-54.

Anon. (1994). Trainers network on the Net. *Training & Development, 48*(8), 35-37.

Anon. (1995). Building a management competency system that yields results, not scorn. *Training Directors' Forum Newsletter, 11*(12), 1-2.

Anon. (1996). 1996 ASTD multimedia software directory. *Technical & Skills Training, 7*(4), 17-20.

Anon. (1996). 1996 industry report: Who's learning what? *Training, 33*(10), 53-65.

Anon. (1996). CBT's untold story. *CBT Solutions,* May/June, 6-12.

Anon. (1996). CD training set offers everything you wanted to know...but never asked. *Information Today, 13*(9), 29.

Anon. (1996). Conversations with the top five: Reviewing the strategies for authoring system vendors. *CBT Solutions,* Jan/Feb, 6-21.

Anon. (1996). Interactive simulation in courseware: A CBT challenge. *CBT Solutions,* Mar/Apr, 33-35.

Anon. (1996). Interactive training series on CD: Coping with organizational change. *Information Today, 13*(5), 43, 50.

Anon. (1996). Multimedia training in the Fortune 1,000. *Training, 33*(9), 53-60.

Anon. (1996). Performance-centered systems: An interview with Paul Johnson and Barry Raybould. *CBT Solutions,* Jan/Feb, 79-83.

Anon. (1996). Swimming the channel. *Training, 33*(8), N-T.

Anon. (1996). The CBT Solutions guide to solutions providers. *CBT Solutions,* Jan/Feb, 32-75.

Armstrong, M. (1995). Measuring work: The vital statistics. *People Management, 1*(19), 34-35.

Aronson, D.T. (1995). Lessons learned in developing an interactive multimedia course for training California peace officers in first aid/CPR. *Journal of Instruction Delivery Systems, 9*(2), 31-34.

Bainbridge, S.V. (1995). You can't teach softskills on a computer...can you? *Journal of Instruction Delivery Systems, 9*(4), 5-12.

Barker, D.I. (1994-95). A technological revolution in higher education. *Journal of Educational Technology Systems, 23*(2), 155-168.

Barron, A.E. (1997). Guidelines for designing Web-based courses. *CBT Solutions,* Mar/Apr, 25-28.

Barron, A.E. and Orwig, G.W. (1995). Digital video and the Internet: A powerful combination. *Journal of Instruction Delivery Systems, 9*(3), 10-12.

Barron, T. (1996). Getting friendly with authoring tools. *Training & Development, 50*(5), 36-46.

Barron, T. (1996). Technical trainers take on multimedia. *Technical & Skills Training, 7*(4), 8-14.

Barron, T. (1997). The new universe of multimedia courseware. *Technical & Skills Training, 8*(4), 8-11.

Benson, G. (1997). A new look at EPSS. *Training & Development, 51*(1), 48-49.

Benson, G.S. and Cheney, S.L. (1996). Best practices in training delivery. *Technical & Skills Training, 7*(7), 14-17.

Berge, Z.L. (1995). Facilitating computer conferencing: Recommendations from the field. *Educational Technology, 35*(1), 22-30.

Bergeron, B.P. (1996). Competency as a paradigm for technology-enabled instruction and evaluation. *Journal of Instruction Delivery Systems, 10*(2), 22-24.

Blalock, R.H. (1995). Using development "shells" for fast and creative multimedia development at American Airlines. *Journal of Instruction Delivery Systems, 9*(3), 3-9.

Blumfield, M. (1997). Learning to share. *Training, 34*(4), 38-42.

Bonello, D. and Cavagnol, R.M. (1996). Computer-based training for loan counselors. *Performance Improvement, 35*(8), 20-24.

Boothman, T. (1995). Ride the wave of innovation: Integrate multimedia into your classroom instruction. *CBT Solutions,* Aug/Sep, 16-19.

Bozeman, W. and Wright, R.H. (1994-95). Simulation applications in educational leadership. *Journal of Educational Technology Systems, 23*(3), 219-231.

Bramble, W.J. and Martin, B.L. (1995). The Florida teletraining project: Military training via two-way compressed video. *American Journal of Distance Education, 9*(1), 6-26.

Briggs, R.O. (1994/1995). The Exemplar project: Using group support systems to improve the learning environment. *Journal of Educational Technology Systems, 23*(3), 277-291.

Brocklesby, J. (1995). Using soft systems methodology to identify competence requirements in HRM. *International Journal of Manpower, 16*(5,6), 70-84.

Brown, J. (1997). Amdahl spin-off rolls out Web-based training tools. *Network World, 14*(9), 42.

Browning, D.L. (1995). High-tech and just in time. *Human Resource Executive, 9*(9), 32-35.

Burgess, G.W. (1996). The design of adult learning around multimedia delivery. *Journal of Interactive Instruction Development, 9*(1), 3-9.

Burns, A. (1997). Multimedia as a quality solution. *Quality Progress, 30*(2), 51-54.

Byers, D.L.; Hilgenberg, C.S.; and Rhodes, D.M. (1995/6). Evaluation of interactive television continuing education programs for health-care professionals. *Journal of Educational Technology Systems, 24*(3), 259-270.

Byham, W.C. and Pescuric, A. (1996). Behavior modeling at the teachable moment. *Training, 33*(12), 50-56.

Campbell, J.O.; Graham, J.; and McCain, D. (1996). Interactive distance learning and job support strategies for soft skills. *Journal of Interactive Instruction Development, 9*(1), 19-21.

Carr, C. and Totzke, L. (1995). The long and winding path (from instructional design to performance technology) Installment VI—Two final tools. *Performance & Instruction, 34*(7), 4-8.

Casey, C. (1996). Incorporating cognitive apprenticeship in multimedia. *Educational Technology Research & Development, 44*(1), 71-84.

Caudron, S. (1996). Wake up to new learning technologies. *Training & Development, 50*(5), 30-35.

Caudron, S. (1996). Your learning technology primer. *Personnel Journal, 75*(6), 119-136.

Cavagnol, R.M. (1996). Painting cars with CD-ROMs. *Performance & Instruction, 35*(3), 24-28.

Cavagnol, R.M. (1996). Painting cars with multimedia. *Journal of Instruction Delivery Systems, 10*(3), 22-28.

Cennamo, K.S. and Dawley, G.W. (1995). Designing interactive video materials for adult learners. *Performance & Instruction, 34*(1), 14-19.

Chapman, B.L. and Allen, R.J. (1994). Teaching problem solving skills using cognitive simulations in a PC-environment. *Journal of Interactive Instruction Development*, 6(4), 24-30.

Charlton, J.M. (1995). The symbiosis of andragogy, interactive courseware and distance education. *Journal of Instruction Delivery Systems*, 9(1), 6-10.

Cichelli, J. (1996). A glueware approach to performance support. *Technical & Skills Training*, 7(6), 20-23.

Clark, R.E. (1994). Media will never influence learning. *Educational Technology Research & Development*, 42(2), 21-29.

Clinton, B.J. (1995). A performance support system for Georgia magistrate court judges. *Journal of Instruction Delivery Systems*, 9(1), 37-40.

Cohen, S. (1997). Intranets uncovered. *Training & Development*, 51(2), 48-50.

Collis, B.A. and Verwijs, C. (1995). A human approach to electronic performance and learning support systems: Hybrid EPSSs. *Educational Technology*, 35(1), 5-21.

Conkright, T.D. and Joliat, J. (1996). Designing programs for multiple configurations: "You mean everyone doesn't have a Pentium or better!" *Journal of Interactive Instruction Development*, 8(3), 8-12.

Costello, J., et al. (1995). Interactive multimedia design: A visual approach. Journal of Interactive *Instruction Development*, 8(2), 3-7.

Crenshaw, D. (1997). 'Net training. *InfoWorld*, 19(9), 61-62.

Crowe, M.H. and Bodine, R.L. (1996). Integrating electronic learning and performance support tools. *CBT Solutions*, May/June, 14-19.

Crowther, E.G. and Jackson, J.T. (1995). An intelligent tutoring system for F-15 flightline troubleshooting. *Journal of Instruction Delivery Systems*, 9(1), 16-22.

Curtin, C. (1997). Getting off to a good start on intranets. *Training & Development*, 51(2), 42-46.

Dahmer, B. (1995). A 12-step program for TBT success. *Training & Development*, 49(3), 56-58.

David, A.G. (1995). How to get what you need (and want) from your multimedia vendor. *Journal of Instruction Delivery Systems*, 9(4), 42-46.

Davis, C. and Cherryhomes, K. (1996). Retrofitting instructor-led training to CBT. *CBT Solutions*, Mar/Apr, 19-24.

Dede, C. (1996). The evolution of distance education: Emerging technologies and distributed learning. *American Journal of Distance Education*, 10(2), 4-36.

Delaney, C. (1995). Trainers and the technology "revolution." *Training & Development*, 49(8), 44-46.

Dennis, A.R. and Valacich, J.S. (1994). Group, sub-group, and nominal group idea generation: New rules for a new media? *Journal of Management*, 20(4), 723-736.

Duggan, B. (1994). A measured approach to microcomputer lab design. *Techtrends*, 39(4), 24-28.

Duke-Moran, C. and Dillon, P. (1996). EPSS: The end state model. *CBT Solutions*, Nov/Dec, 30-33.

Dulworth, M.R. and Shea, R. (1995). Six ways technology improves training. *HRMagazine*, 40(5), 33-36.

Dulworth, M.R. (1996). Interactive multimedia learning systems. *Journal of Instruction Delivery Systems*, 10(3), 29-35.

Dulworth, M.R. and Carney, J. (1996). Improve training with interactive multimedia. *Info-Line*, Jan.; 20.

Elkeles, T. (1996). A learning center on the Web. *CBT Solutions*, Nov/Dec, 20-25.

Farkas, D.F. (1997). This buys me what? *Training*, 34(2), A6-A9.

Fenwick, M. and De Cieri, H. (1995). Building an integrated approach to performance management using critical incident technique. *Asia Pacific Journal of Human Resources*, 33(3), 76-91.

Filipczak, B. (1994). Trainers on the Net. *Training, 31*(12), 42-51.

Filipczak, B. (1995). On the trail of better multimedia. *Training, 32*(11), 56-62.

Filipczak, B. (1996). Engaged! The nature of computer interactivity. *Training, 33*(11), 52-58.

Filipczak, B. (1996). To ISD or not ISD? *Training, 33*(3), 73-74.

Filipczak, B. (1996). Training on intranets: The hope and the hype. *Training, 33*(9), 24-32.

Filipczak, B. (1997). Finally, an EPSS status report. *Training, 34*(5), 119-120.

Fleischman, J. (1996). The web: New venue for adult education. *Adult Learning, 8*(1), 17-18.

Franci, J. (1994). Virtual reality: An overview. *Techtrends, 39*(1), 23-26.

Freitag, E.T. and Sullivan, H.J. (1995). Matching learner preference to amount of instruction: An alternative form of learner control. *Educational Technology Research & Development, 43*(2), 5-14.

Friedlander, P. (1996). Competency-driven, component-based curriculum architecture. *Performance & Instruction, 35*(2), 14-21.

Fritz, M. (1994). The rise of CD-ROM. *Training, 31*(9), 44-49.

Furst-Bowe, J.A. (1996). An analysis of the competencies needed by trainers to use computer-based technologies and distance learning systems. *Performance Improvement Quarterly, 9*(4), 57-78.

Galagan, P.A. (1994). Performance support systems: A conversation with Gloria Gery. *Technical & Skills Training, 5*(3), 6-10.

Galagan, P.A. (1994). Think performance. *Training & Development, 48*(3), 47-51.

Galbreath, J. (1995). Multimedia on the network: Has its time come? *Educational Technology, 35*(4), 44-51.

Gallagher, M. (1996). Why the web browser is the clearest window to EPSS. *CBT Solutions*, Nov/Dec, 15-18.

Gallagher, M.P. (1996). Is CD-ROM a dinosaur? *CBT Solutions*, May/June, 24-27.

Gant, L.P. (1995). Use of emerging technologies: Training troops around the world. *Performance & Instruction, 34*(1), 11-13.

Gant, L.P. (1996). Lessons in developing distance learning. *Performance & Instruction, 35*(2), 22-25.

Garland, V.E. and Loranger, A. (1995/6). The medium and the message: Interactive television and distance education programs for adult learners. *Journal of Educational Technology Systems, 24*(3), 249-257.

Garmonsway, A. and Wellin, M. (1995). Creating the right natural chemistry. *People Management, 1*(19), 36-39.

Golas, K.C.; Fredrickson, R.C.; and Negri, M.A. (1995). Computer-based English language training for the Royal Saudi Naval Forces. *Journal of Interactive Instruction Development, 7*(4), 3-9.

Golub, S. Z. (1995). Multimedia: The future of adult learning. *Career Planning and Adult Development Journal, 11*(2), 15-21.

Gordon, J. and Hequet, M. (1997). Live and in person. *Training, 34*(3), 24-31.

Gorsline, K. (1996). A competency profile for human resources: No more shoemaker's children. *Human Resource Management, 35*(1), 53-66.

Grantham, T. (1997). Canadian bank uses multimedia to train employees. *Computerworld, 31*(7), 63, 65.

Green, E.E.; Cook, P.F.; and Bolt, L. (1996). Fitting new technologies into traditional classrooms: two case studies in the design of improved learning facilities. *Educational Technology, 36*(4), 27-38.

Griffiths, J. and Degner, A. (1994/1995). Training for instructional uses of multimedia at San Juan College: Toward the campus of the future. *Journal of Educational Technology Systems, 23*(4), 337-352.

Guilar, J. (1994). Instructional technology versus the traditional teacher: An evaluation. *Journal of Instruction Delivery Systems, 8*(2), 17-20.

Hall, B. (1996). Easing into multimedia. *Training & Development, 50*(4), 61-62.

Hall, B. (1996). Ten training mistakes to avoid. *Training & Development, 50*(7), 55.

Hamblen, M. (1997). CD-ROMs have tech trainees playing games. *Computerworld, 31*(9), 41-42.

Hammond, R. (1996). Internal networks: The inside story. *People Management, 2*(11), 22-27.

Hawkins, D.T. (1997). Web-based training for online retrieval: An idea whose time is coming. *Online, 21*(3), 68-69.

Henderson, L. (1996). Instructional design of interactive multimedia: A cultural critique. *Educational Technology Research & Development, 44*(4), 85-104.

Hequet, M. (1997). How does multimedia change training? *Presentations, 11*(2), A20-A22.

Hequet, M. (1997). How does multimedia change training? *Training, 34*(2), A20-A22.

Hillis, D.R. (1994). Formulating training needs for a new technology using a computer-based simulation supported by artificial intelligence. *Journal of Industrial Teacher Education, 31*(3), 66-78.

Hoffman, J.S. (1996). Performance support for complex procedures. *Journal of Instruction Delivery Systems, 10*(1), 3-9.

Horney, N.F. and Koonce, R. (1995). The missing piece in reengineering. *Training & Development, 49*(12), 37-43.

Horowitz, A.S. (1997). 'Net train, net gain? *Computerworld, 31*(5), 63-66.

Hudzina, M.; Rowley, K.; and Wager, W. (1996). Electronic performance support technology: Defining the domain. *Performance Improvement Quarterly, 9*(1), 36-48.

Hyde, J. and Montgomery, A. (1994). Guidelines for CMI interoperability: The aviation industry steps forward. *Journal of Interactive Instruction Development, 7*(1), 3-12.

Ignico, A.A. (1994/1995). A comparison of videotape and teacher-directed instruction on knowledge, performance, and assessment of fundamental motor skills. *Journal of Educational Technology Systems, 23*(4), 363-368.

Jackson, M.A. (1996). Employing art of storytelling. *Computing Canada, 22*(18), 41.

Jategaonkar, V.A. and Babu, A.J.G. (1995). Interactive multimedia instructional systems: A conceptual framework. *Journal of Instruction Delivery Systems, 9*(4), 24-29.

Johnson, P. (1996). The future of multimedia in training. *CBT Solutions*, Mar/Apr, 36-43.

Jonassen, D.H.; Campbell, J.P.; and Davidson, M.E. (1994). Learning with media: Restructuring the debate. *Educational Technology Research & Development, 42*(2), 31-39.

Kearsley, G.; Lynch, W.; and Wizer, D. (1995). The effectiveness and impact of online learning in graduate education. *Educational Technology, 35*(6), 37-42.

Keith, J.D. and Payton, E.S. (1995). The new face of training. *Training & Development, 49*(2), 49-51.

Kemske, F. (1996). Mid-morning after the dawn of EPSS. *CBT Solutions*, Sep/Oct, 1, 6-12.

Kimmerling, G. (1995). Surveying the suppliers' market. *Training & Development, 49*(10), 34-39.

King, J. (1997). Teaching over the 'Net. *Computerworld, 31*(20), 59-61.

Kiss, S. (1996). Various methods compared. *Computing Canada, 22*(18), 38.

Knerr, B.W., et al. (1994). Research in the use of virtual environment technology to train dismounted soldiers. *Journal of Interactive Instruction Development, 6*(4), 9-20.

Kozma, R.B. (1994). Will media influence learning? Reframing the debate. *Educational Technology Research & Development, 42*(2), 7-19.

Kroeker, K.L. (1996). Multimedia training multiples in corporate classrooms. *CD-ROM Professional, 9*(3), 14-15.

Kruse, K. (1997). Five levels of Internet-based training. *Training & Development, 51*(2), 60-61.

Kruse, K. and Feldstein, M. (1997). Exploring multimedia Internet-based training. *Training & Development, 51*(3), 55-56.

Laabs, J.J. (1996). Duke's newest power tool. *Personnel Journal, 75*(6), 44-52.

Lane, T. (1995). The paperless ship. *Training & Development, 49*(8), 59-60.

LeBleu, R. and Sobkowiak, R. (1995). New workforce competency models: Getting the IS staff up to warp speed. *Information Systems Management, 12*(3), 7-12.

Lee, W.W. and Mamone, R.A. (1995). Design criteria that make tests objective. *Journal of Instruction Delivery Systems, 9*(3), 18-22.

Levin, S.A. (1994). Basics of electronic performance support systems. *Info-Line*, Dec.; 12.

Lhotka, P.H., et al. (1994). Lessons learned from a CBT development team. *Journal of Interactive Instruction Development, 7*(1), 23-30.

Litsikas, M. (1996). Take training to a new dimension. *Quality, 35*(1), 50-52.

Lozano, C. (1997). New methods to control and access information. *CBT Solutions*, Mar/Apr, 46-48.

MacKnight, C.B. and Fitzgerald, J.E. (1995). The Internet: Transforming the way business works. *Journal of Instruction Delivery Systems, 9*(1), 11-15.

Majchrzak, T.L. (1996). Developing multimedia courseware for the Internet-Java versus Shockwave. *Journal of Interactive Instruction Development, 9*(1), 16-18.

Mansfield, R.S. (1996). Building competency models: Approaches for HR professionals. *Human Resource Management, 35*(1), 7-18.

Marquardt, M.J. (1996). Cyberlearning: New possibilities for HRD. *Training & Development, 50*(11), 56-57.

Martin, B.L. and Bramble, W.J. (1996). Designing effective video teletraining instruction: The Florida teletraining project. *Educational Technology Research & Development, 44*(1), 85-99.

Masie, E. (1997). Seizing your intranet. *Training & Development, 51*(2), 51-52.

Mattoon, J.S. (1996). Modeling and simulation: A rationale for implementing new training technologies. *Educational Technology, 36*(4), 17-26.

Mauldin, M. (1996). The development of computer-based multimedia: Is a rainforest the same place as a jungle? *Techtrends, 41*(3), 15-19.

Mauldin, M.S. (1996). The unanticipated effects of an electronic performance support system. *Journal of Instruction Delivery Systems, 10*(3), 3-7.

McCollum, T. (1997). Handy tools for training. *Nation's Business, 85*(4), 49-50.

McGee, M.K. (1996). Multimedia-based training on the rise. *Informationweek, (607),* 109.

McGrath, S. (1997). 'Net institute helps skills crisis. *InfoWorld Canada, 22*(3), 25.

McHale, J. (1996). Late arrivals cause a multimedia sensation. *People Management, 2*(3), 54.

McLagan, P. (1996). Great ideas revisited: Competency models. *Training & Development, 50*(1). 60-64.

McNerney, D. and Briggins, A. (1995). Competency assessment gains favor among trainers. *HR Focus, 72*(6), 19.

Meilach, D.Z. (1995). The laptop trainer. *Training, 32*(3), 67-72.

Merrill, K. (1996). Oracle joins crowded Net training fray. *Computer Reseller News, (708),* 44.

Miller, B. (1995). A system design model for an electronic performance support system. *Performance & Instruction, 34*(7), 24-26.

Minton-Eversole, T. (1997). IBT training: Truths behind the hype. *Technical & Skills Training,* 8(1), 15-19.

Mirabile, R.J. (1995). Use competency-based strategies to meet business needs. *Human Resources Professional,* 8(5), 12-17.

Misanchuk, E.R. and Schwier, R.A. (1996). Benefits and pitfalls of using HTML as a CD-ROM development tool. *Journal of Interactive Development,* 8(4), 3-14.

Mitra, A. (1994). "Instructor-Effect" in determining effectiveness and attitude towards technology-assisted teaching: Report of a case study. *Journal of Instruction Delivery Systems,* 8(3), 15-21.

Mize, C.D. (1996). Desktop video communication: A primer. *Techtrends,* 41(6), 44-47.

Mollick, J. (1995). EPSS case study for letter sorting equipment. *Journal of Interactive Instruction Development,* 7(4), 15-20.

Morgan, J. (1996). Shell dips into multimedia. *Computing Canada,* 22(18), 39.

Morris, D. (1996). Using competency development tools as a strategy for change in the human resources function: A case study. *Human Resource Management,* 35(1), 35-51.

Mugg, J.C. (1996). Team-building strategies for multimedia teams. *Performance & Instruction,* 35(6), 10-11.3

Munger, P.D. (1996). A guide to high-tech training delivery: Part I. *Training & Development,* 50(12), 55-57.

Munger, P.D. (1996). Training delivery in the chemical process industry. *Technical & Skills Training,* 7(6), 17-19.

Munger, P.D. (1997). High-tech training delivery methods: When to use them. *Training & Development,* 51(1), 46-47.

Murphy, C. (1996). Working with outside vendors to develop multimedia training programs. *Performance & Instruction,* 35(2), 26-29.

Nicholson, A.Y.W. and Ngai, J.Y.K. (1995/1996). Converting a traditional multimedia kit into an interactive video CD-ROM. *Journal of Educational Technology Systems,* 24(3), 235-248.

Nicolo, E. and Sapio, B. (1996). Structural analysis of the global multimedia scenario: Technological, market, environmental, and regulatory issues. *Journal of Instruction Delivery Systems,* 10(1); 17-27.

Northrup, P.T. (1995). Concurrent formative evaluation: Guidelines and implications for multimedia designers. *Educational Technology,* 35(6), 24-31.

O'Connell, S.E. (1996). CD-ROMs offer practical advantages for HR. *HRMagazine,* 41(11), 35-38.

O'Herron, P. and Simonsen, P. (1995). Career development gets a charge at Sears Credit. *Personnel Journal,* 74(5), 103-106.

Okonski, S. (1996). The world is an authoring system. *CBT Solutions,* Mar/Apr, 25-28.

Oktem, U.G. (1996). Using interactive multimedia training in TQEM systems and applications. *Total Quality Environmental Management,* 5(3), 89-99.

Overmyer-Day, L. and Benson, G. (1996). Training success stories. *Training & Development,* 50(6), 24-29.

Parks, E. and Preston, J.R. (1996). Before you buy...12 critical questions to ask before you purchase training software. *CBT Solutions,* Jan/Feb, 26-31.

Parry, S.B. (1996). The quest for competencies. *Training,* 33(7), 48-56.

Patrick, E. (1996). Distributed curriculum development environments: Techniques and tools. *Journal of Interactive Instruction Development,* 8(4), 26-34.

Paulus-Shufflebarger, K.L. (1996). A primer on online documentation. *Technical & Skills Training,* 7(1), 23-25.

Pearson, L. (1996). Get connected with cutting-edge presentation tools. *Training, 33*(9), A-R.

Penaranda, E.A. (1995). Teletraining: From the mailbox to cyberspace. *Journal of Instruction Delivery Systems, 9*(2), 11-16.

Pool, T.S.; Blanchard, S.M.; and Hale, S.A. (1995). From over the Internet: Users discuss a new direction for learning. *Techtrends, 4*(1), 24-28.

Quinlan, L.R. (1996). The digital classroom. *Techtrends, 41*(6), 6-8.

Raelin, J.A. and Colledge, A.S. (1995). From generic to organic competencies. *Human Resource Planning, 18*(3), 24-33.

Raes, D.W. (1995). A methodology for selection of training to apply computer-based instruction. *Journal of Interactive Instruction Development, 7*(3), 31-37.

Raimy, E. (1996). Star performers. *Human Resource Executive, 10*(8), 1, 22-25.

Rakow, J. (1997). Networking multimedia training. *Training, 34*(3), 61-65.

Ramsey, B. and Murphy, P. (1996). Human factors considerations in multimedia courseware development. *Journal of Interactive Instruction Development, 9*(1), 10-15.

Rand, A. (1996). Technology transforms training. *HR Focus, 73*(11), 11-13.

Rao, S.S. (1995). Putting fun back into learning. *Training, 32*(8), 44-48.

Ray, R.D.; Gogoberidze, T.; and Begiashvili, V. (1995). Adaptive computerized instruction. *Journal of Instruction Delivery Systems, 9*(3), 28-31.

Raybould, B. (1995). Development tools for EPSS. *Journal of Interactive Instruction Development, 7*(3), 25-30.

Raybould, B. (1995). Making EPSS work for your organization. *Info-Line*, Jan.; 20.

Reynolds, A. (1995). The basics: The trainer's Internet. *Technical & Skills Training, 6*(2), 25-26.

Ricci, K.E. (1994). The use of computer-based videogames in knowledge acquisition and retention. *Journal of Interactive Instruction Development, 7*(1), 17-22.

Richman, T. (1995). Identifying future leaders. *Harvard Business Review, 73*(6), 15-16.

Roblyer, M.D.; Dozier-Henry, O.; and Burnette, A.P. (1996). Technology and multicultural education: The "uneasy alliance." *Educational Technology, 36*(3), 5-12.

Rosenof, R. (1996). Multiple delivery strategies and changing business demands. *CBT Solutions*, May/June, 28-32.

Rossett, A. and Barnett, J. (1996). Designing under the influence. *Training, 33*(12), 34-42.

Rowe, C. (1995). Clarifying the use of competence and competency models in recruitment, assessment and staff development. *Industrial & Commercial Training, 27*(11), 12-17.

Shotsberger, P.G. (1996). Instructional uses of the World Wide Web: Exemplars and precautions. *Educational Technology, 36*(2), 47-50.

Silverstein, N. (1997). Duracell's integrated training approach. *CBT Solutions*, Mar/Apr, 49-52.

Smith, K. (1995). Making the transition to EPSS. *CBT Solutions*, Aug/Sep, 8-10.

Smith, M. and Gustafson, K. (1995). Using a barcode reader with interactive videodiscs. *Techtrends, 40*(1), 29-32.

Smith, V.C. (1994). An upgrade for testing. *Human Resource Executive, 8*(14), 41-43.

Spencer, B.S. (1995). Technology—it's all in the sales pitch! *Performance & Instruction, 34*(4), 35-36.

Srtazewski, L. (1995). Making the Net work. *Human Resource Executive, 9*(7), 40-43.

Starr, R.M. and William, D. (1996). Educational uses of the Internet: An exploratory survey. *Educational Technology, 36*(5), 19-28.

Stevens, G. and Stevens, E. (1996). The truth about EPSS. *Training & Development, 50*(6), 59-61.

Stevens, L. (1996). The intranet: your newest training tool? *Personnel Journal, 75*(7), 26-32.

Stewart, R.D. (1995). Distance learning technology. *New Directions for Adult and Continuing Education,* (67), 11-18.

Stewart, T.A. (1994). The netplex: It's a new silicon valley. *Fortune, 129*(5), 98-104.

Sykes, D.J. and Swinscoe, P.C. (1995). Digital video for multimedia, what are the alternatives? *Journal of Interactive Instruction Development, 7*(3), 9-19.

Telg, R.W. (1996). The roles of television production specialists in distance education programming. *American Journal of Distance Education, 10*(1), 50-61.

Tessmer, M. and Jonassen, D. (1994). Evaluating computer-based training for repurposing to multimedia: A case study. *Performance & Instruction, 33*(7), 3-8.

Tetzeli, R. (1994). The Internet and your business. *Fortune, 129*(5), 86-96.

Tetzeli, R. (1996). Getting your company's Internet strategy right. *Fortune, 133*(5), 72-78.

Theurmer, K.E. (1995). World class. *Human Resource Executive, 9*(13), 26-30.

Tolhurst, D. (1995). Hypertext, hypermedia, multimedia defined? *Educational Technology. 35*(2), 21-26.

Toohey, S. (1995). Competency-based management education—what does it have to offer? *Asia Pacific Journal of Human Resources, 33*(2), 118-126.

Varnadoe, S. and Barron, A.E. (1994). Designing electronic performance support systems. *Journal of Interactive Instruction Development, 6*(3), 12-17.

Waldman, D.P. (1996). Interactive multimedia: Measuring the ROI. *Journal of Interactive Instruction Development, 8*(3), 18-20.

Warren, T. (1996). What, whys, and hows: A web primer for trainers. *Technical & Skills Training, 7*(7), 7.

Webb, W. (1997). High-tech in the heartland. *Training, 34*(5), 50-56.

Webb, W. (1997). Multimedia training on a budget. *Training, 34*(2), A12-A18.

Webster, J. (1996). Don't train in vain. *Software Magazine, 16*(9), 99-103.

Weiss, E. (1994). Is your CBT people-literate? *Performance & Instruction, 33*(2), 3-6.

Weiss-Morris, L. (1996). Just-in-time training: How one company blends LAN-based CBTs with instructor-led classes. *CBT Solutions,* Mar/Apr, 5-11.

Whiteside, J.A. and Whiteside, M.F. (1996). EPSS makes good ROI sense. *Journal of Instruction Delivery Systems, 10*(1), 10-13.

Wood, D. (1996). A framework for re-engineering traditional training: Interactive training and electronic performance support. *Performance Improvement, 35*(8), 14-18.

Wulf, K. (1996). Training via the Internet: Where are we? *Training & Development, 50*(5), 50-55.

Yang, C.S. and Moore, D.M. (1995/1996). Designing hypermedia systems for instruction. *Journal of Educational Technology Systems, 24*(1), 3-30.

Zemke, R. and Armstrong, J. (1996). A bluffer's guide to multimedia. *Training, 33*(6), 36-44.

Zemke, R. and Armstrong, J. (1996). Evaluating multimedia developers. *Training, 33*(11), 32-38.

Zemke, R. and Armstrong, J. (1996). Evaluating multimedia. *Training, 33*(8), 48-52.

Zemke, R. and Armstrong, J. (1996). Sorting "for reals" from "wannabes." *Training, 33*(11), 34.

Zielinski, D. (1994). New technologies offer trainers opportunity for influence. *Training Directors' Forum Newsletter, 10*(6), 1-3.

Zinno, V. (1995). The message of multimedia. *Human Resource Executive, 9*(2), 31-34.

GLOSSARY

Please note that the following lists of learning technologies are not meant to be exhaustive. New electronic technologies for learning are being introduced every day.

Learning Technologies Defined
Electronic technologies that deliver information and facilitate the development of skills and knowledge.

Presentation Methods
Audio: One-way delivery of live or recorded sound.

CBT: A general term used to describe any learning event that uses computers as the primary distribution method; typically used to refer primarily to text-based, computer-delivered training.

Electronic performance support system (EPSS): An integrated computer application that uses any combination of expert systems, hypertext, embedded animation, hypermedia, or a combination of these to help a user to perform a task in real time quickly and with minimal of support by other people.

Electronic text: The dissemination of text via electronic means.

Groupware: An integrated computer application that supports collaborative group efforts through the sharing of calendars for project management and scheduling, collective document preparation, e-mail handling, shared database access, electronic meetings, and other activities.

Interactive TV: One-way video combined with two-way audio or other electronic response systems.

Multimedia: A computer application that uses any combination of text, graphics, audio, animation, full-motion video, or a combination of these. Interactive multimedia enables the user to control various aspects of the training such as content sequence.

Online help: A computer application that provides online assistance to employees.

Teleconferencing: The instantaneous exchange of audio, video, or text among two or more or individuals or groups at two or more locations.

3D modeling/virtual reality: A computer application that provides an interactive, immersive, and three-dimensional learning experience through fully functional, realistic models.

Video: One-way delivery of live or recorded full-motion pictures.

Distribution Methods
Cable TV: The transmission of television signals via cable technology.

CD-ROM: A format and system for recording, storing, and retrieving electronic information on a compact disk that is read using an optical drive.

Electronic mail (e-mail): The exchange of messages through computers.

Extranet: A collaborative network that uses Internet technology to link organizations with their suppliers, customers, or other organizations that share common goals or information.

Internet: A loose confederation of computer networks around the world that are connected through several primary networks.

Intranet: A general term describing any network contained within an organization; used to refer primarily to networks that use Internet technology.

Local area network (LAN): A network of computers sharing the resources of a single processor or server within a relatively small geographic area.

Satellite TV: The transmission of television signals via satellites.

Tactile gear/simulator: A device or system that replicates or imitates a real device or system.

Voice mail: An automated, electronic telephone answering system.

Wide area network (WAN): A network of computers sharing the resources of one or more processors or servers over a relatively large geographic area.

World Wide Web: All the resources and users on the Internet using the hypertext transport protocol (HTTP—a set of rules for exchanging files)

Instructional Methods[4]

Case study: A technique for practicing problem solving using a hypothetical scenario. It requires reading, study, analysis, discussion, and a free exchange of ideas as well as decision making and the selling of decisions to others.

Demonstration: A basic instructional method where an operation or task is performed in front of a learner, thereby showing the learner what to do and how to do it.

Expert panel: A group of experts, often with diverse opinions or positions, sharing their ideas with each other and with an audience.

Games: Contests and matches used in training to develop management skills, improve technical performance, foster cooperation and teamwork, and improve decision-making ability.

Group discussion: Two or more individuals considering a question in open and informal debate in order to facilitate learning.

Lecture: A semiformal discourse in which a person presents a series of events, facts, concepts, or principles to the learner. Learners participate mainly as listeners and questioners.

Practical exercise: The opportunity to demonstrate skill proficiency without the requirements of a graded test.

Programmed instruction: A method of self-instruction in which trainees work through a carefully sequenced and pretested series of steps leading to the acquisition of knowledge or skills representing the instructional objectives.

Reading: The acquisition of information in written form.

Role play: An interactive method of instruction that involves the spontaneous dramatization of a situation by two or more individuals for the purpose of practicing interpersonal skills within the context of the workplace.

Simulation: A technique that imitates operations and responses to problems and situations to test the ability of a person, system, or procedure to overcome obstacles and meet variations. Advanced simulations can create an artificial environment that closely emulates the actual workplace.

We would like your input on these definitions and distinctions. Send comments to panderson@astd.org.

---

[4] *Adapted from The Human Resources Glossary, William R. Tracey.*

APPENDIX A ARTICLES ON "THE FUTURE OF LEARNING TECHNOLOGIES"

To complement the quantitative data that were collected for this study, researchers gave all of the study's participants an opportunity to write a short article on the future of learning technologies. The focus of these articles was intentionally left open ended in order to facilitate divergent thinking. In addition, the authors did not tailor their articles to fit with the content of the book. Instead, they were encouraged to write from their own perspective and to focus on whatever facet of learning technologies they felt strongly about. These articles are intended to be thought provoking and may not always agree with the exact findings of this study.

We have also added to this section a recent article from *Training & Development* magazine because it summarizes the opinions of many experts in the field and describes their vision of the future.

STRATEGIC PARTNERSHIPS FOR TRAINERS: THE KEY TO EXCELLENCE IN LEARNING TECHNOLOGY
By Caitlin Curtin, President and CEO, Luminare

New and diverse tools are flooding the training world every day, bringing just-in-time training and performance support within the reach of most organizations. These new technologies also bring new challenges to the trainer. The plethora of current electronic training tools includes such items as Web-based training, electronic performance support systems, online collaboration, online mentoring, CD-ROMs, and now even DVD.

Until recently, a trainer who was using learning technologies to solve performance problems and skill and knowledge deficiencies had to know enough about computers to be sure that the training program would run on the organization's computers. By and large, the bulk of a trainer's work in learning technologies was limited to determining when one of a few commonly used learning technologies was appropriate, and then developing or buying a stand-alone program. For most trainers, however, those days are over.

Today's training professional is typically being asked to improve employee skills and performance and use technology to minimize the disruption to the employee's work schedule. In a typical organization, training managers are actively buying and developing CD-ROM training programs and are thinking of ways to use the company's intranet or client-server network to distribute training programs. Other HRD activities that may soon be conducted over the intranet include user administration, interactive media development, performance support interventions, decentralized content development, mentoring, and online collaboration.

All of these activities, while sharing the general purpose of enabling employees, involve breadth and depth of knowledge in tasks both inside and outside of the training discipline. A common mistake of training professionals is to assume that they are responsible for acquiring all of the necessary skills. This misconception leads to mediocre interventions and pedestrian work.

The training discipline, with its grounding in instructional design, adult education, cognitive psychology, and learning theory, to name a few, gives trainers the background to analyze performance problems, identify competency deficiencies, and create elegant solutions. Like a conductor of an orchestra, our job is not to play all of the notes, but to specify when, how, and which instruments should be played, making

use of the talents and skills of the musicians to create a harmonious sound. Trainers have often provided coaching, facilitation services, and, with a varying degree of quality, materials and graphics development. (The trainers who develop the best quality materials often have a background in graphic design, media production, and other creative disciplines.)

Most phenomenally successful enterprises (those with stellar products, excellent service, and ascending revenues) are achieving success through strategic partnerships. In a strategic partnership, all parties bring their strongest attributes to the table, and together the whole is greater than the parts. For example, when US Electrical Motors saw an opportunity to sell testing technology in addition to its motors, it called upon DEI Inc. to supply the company with testing devices. By adding DEI's expertise to its service package, US Electric increased quality and value for its customers, received higher prices, and increased its sales volume by 20 percent—all without adding extra sales and marketing expenses.

Training professionals too should see creating strategic partnerships with internal and external technology providers as a critical element of their job. By aligning themselves with experts in other disciplines such as information technology, graphics, and human interface design, trainers can extend their capabilities and become more innovative.

Some people may ask, "Why can't the training department manage the entire process from needs analysis through program implementation?" The answer is simple: New technologies that can be used to solve training problems are emerging too rapidly, are too numerous, and are too diverse for training professionals to consider on their own. For example, a training manager thinking about implementing online course registration, online training, online performance support, or collaborative groupware over the company's intranet will need to think about system and information architecture, platforms, quality assurance, beta testing, bandwidth, off-the-shelf tools versus custom development, human interface, screen design, graphics limitations, content templates, editorial style, programming, and deployment.

Rather than staffing with specialists deeply skilled in each of those areas or, worse yet, trying to turn an instructional media developer into a Java expert, a training manager is best served to partner with others for initial design and development, then later contract out for technical support and other services. These partners can be internal or external. The primary goal is to keep the training staff focused on those areas where they add the most value. This also frees up training staff to be more proactive consultants to the business and, in some cases, figure out how to sell training innovations to others. Occasionally, other business units can provide all or partial program funding.

Trainers should continue to focus on providing such core services as needs analysis, task analysis, instructional design, coaching, presentation, evaluation, and, to a small degree, materials development. Trainers should also read training and related industry publications and devour any and all case study histories of interesting technology implementations that supported learning. (And those aren't just technologies already identified as "learning technologies!") Truly excellent trainers will also partner with systems analysts, programmers, media developers, graphic artists, and others to design and develop more complex projects.

These partners can be specialty vendors, freelancers, or other business units such as information systems and corporate communications. These partners, especially ones at the cutting edge of their own discipline, will not necessarily have any training experience. Chosen with care, however, partners who will collaborate with trainers and use their various disciplines' traditions and strengths can produce innovative, elegant, and efficient solutions to business performance problems.

A Guide to Multimedia

in the Next Millennium

Has multimedia really undergone a transformation? Or does it just
have a sleeker facade? Eight industry pundits scratch beneath the
surface to find out what's new, what's different, and what lies ahead for multimedia training.

F orget dry, text-only training manuals. They've gone the way of the dinosaurs. Current training is multisensory. It's engaging. It takes risks. Trainees learn by doing, seeing, and hearing. They learn on their own time, wherever and whenever they choose. Multimedia technologies, such as audio and video, are breathing new life into training and creating more opportunities for learning.

But let's get real: Is cutting-edge multimedia training feasible for your small, resource-strained department? And, more importantly, do you really need to bother with all of the technological mumbo-jumbo? The answer to both of those questions is an emphatic yes, especially if you want to make your career stronger, your training more productive, and your department more valuable.

In our quest to learn about the true state of multimedia for training, we interviewed a diverse group of top-level executives from such well-known companies as CBT Systems, InFocus, Multimedia Learning, Andersen Consulting, Macromedia, ExecuTrain, Gartner Group, and Aimtech. Each expert had a unique perspective, whether from hands-on experience or big-picture knowledge.

The interviews provide valuable insight into what multimedia training means now, what will be possible in the future, and how the changes will affect the training profession.

BY SACHA COHEN

Paul Johnson, CEO
Multimedia Learning
Irving, Texas
800.870.6608

Company profile: Multimedia Learning sells off-the-shelf training products, software tools for technology-based course development, and consulting talent to develop custom training programs.

What are some emerging multimedia trends?

State-of-the-art multimedia is better than most people think. For example, real-time coaching can be implemented with audio-streaming technology. The first time that I saw the use of coaching in a multimedia course was nearly a year ago at First Union Bank. In the training program, an icon pops up in the corner of the screen and, if you click on the icon, a video of a real teller starts to run. Think how valuable that is for personalized training.

One of the biggest challenges for trainers is keeping ahead of the curve. Technology is being developed in such short cycle times that trainers aren't even close to keeping up.

There is a trend towards new ways of managing and reusing content, accomplished by *chunking*. That means that content is in small granules of information.

Another breakthrough is cross-platform capability. Browser technology has dealt with that limitation very well. Now, corporations with multiple computer platforms can use browsers to deliver training.

How has multimedia changed?

CBT served its purpose and was cost-effective, but it was ugly. Now, we have the tools to do very sophisticated instructional design, such as role play and simulation. In combination with those, we have nice support tools, such as glossaries, reference guides, and notepads built into the instruction that add value to learning.

What's driving better multimedia?

Companies are in pain from competition and time-to-market pressure. Products are coming to market much faster than before and are more complex. Traditional training methods don't work for these kinds of products. For example, banks are rolling out new products every two to three months. The classroom paradigm is collapsing under the weight [of such pressures].

What are your thoughts on the future?

There will be a major shift from event-based learning to technology-based training. It has to do with combining learning and doing.

You will learn, but you may not *know* that you are learning. It will fundamentally change the way we learn.

Reinhard Ziegler, managing partner,
performance design and development
Andersen Consulting
Dallas
214.853.1000

Company profile: Anderson Consulting is a leading global management and technology consulting firm whose mission is to help its clients change to be more successful. The firm works with clients from a wide range of industries to align their people, processes and technology with their strategy to achieve best business performance.

How is multimedia evolving?

I think that we've seen a significant evolution in the past few years in the quality of tools that have been developed. For example, authorware continues to improve in terms of sophistication and ease of use. That puts a lot more power in the hands of less-experienced developers, so it's not as daunting to create multimedia programs.

Are there any new learning models?

We believe that training should look and feel like work.

You have to create a multimedia environment that helps people learn, that supports them while they are doing the work, and that allows them to innovate while they're working. For example, one of our clients is a rapidly growing financial services company that needs to bring new MBAs up to speed as quickly as possible so they can make good business decisions. We built a business simulator that models that entire part of the business in software and multimedia. That's a whole new world of learning, much like a flight simulator. It's an open, discovery environ-

"The biggest innovation will be in the area of instructional design. As the demand for Web-based training increases, training suppliers will be forced to redesign their content. New design models will result in the creation of learning objects or mini tutorials that can be taken either independently or strung together to form an entire course or curriculum. With that flexible architecture, [trainees] can take pre-tests or needs assessments, which automatically present a personalized curriculum using content from a database of learning objects."

—Kevin Kruse, president
Advanced Consulting
Green Brook, New Jersey

MULTIMEDIA TRENDS

Technology alters the way training is conducted and vice versa. In the future, technology and training will be interdependent, with mutable boundaries and unlimited potential. Here are some trends that will shape the future.

The Medium: changes in the way that training will be delivered

- Java programming language
- streaming audio and video
- chunking
- hybrid delivery
- coaching software
- cross-platform capability
- the Internet and intranets
- business simulation technology
- computer-managed instruction
- push technology
- bandwidth improvements
- virtual reality
- data compression
- DVD
- CD-ROM
- MMX computer chip.

The Message: changes in learning and training methods

- technology-based learning
- collaborative learning
- virtual teams
- more learner control
- just-in-time learning
- personalized training
- anytime, anyplace learning
- soft skills training.

ment—as opposed to the older world of CBT, which was very linear.

A business simulator mimics the complexity and degree of interactivity that you would have on the job. In the program, an employee does research, analyzes the business case, and presents business findings to a lending board, which is captured in individual video clips. Based on your level of diligence, you are told to do other things. You can even get 'thrown out' of the meeting if you're not prepared.

Trainees' responses to the program have been superb. You should feel like you're at work, not in training. You should get sweaty palms. Gone are the days of training as a safe place in which no one knows what you are doing. You have to give trainees the opportunity to learn by doing. The entire pace of learning is changing. Training and learning have to move at the speed of work. That means smaller chunks of knowledge, and better and tighter design.

Any words of wisdom?

It's very important for people to be broadly literate in the available technologies. To some extent, corporate trainers and developers are at a disadvantage. They are often asked to write a symphony when they haven't heard music. Learn as much as you can now. Go to the media buffet and snack.

The good news in general is that we're going to see instructional design that is much stronger in its usability and much more focused on understanding users. I think that we can learn something from marketing—for example, testing. Learners know what's best for them, so we need to transfer control to learners.

We operate dynamically, making decisions in real time and reacting to the consequences of those decisions. I think that the trend is for training to reflect that behavior.

Randy Cox, vice president of engineering for the Learning Division
Macromedia
San Francisco
800.326.2128

Company profile: A leading provider of cross-platform software tools for digital media creation and publishing.

What is the current status of multimedia for training?

Interactive multimedia has proven itself over the last decade to be a critical part of organizations' training efforts. The bulk of interactive multimedia training applications are still currently traditional computer-based training, delivered on CD-ROM, over a LAN, or on dedicated PCs. Over the years, the multimedia training industry has settled on a few standard technologies and time-tested tools, including Macromedia's Authorware, which has been the leader in interactive multimedia authoring for training and learning for almost 10 years.

We believe the advent of intranets and the Internet opens the door to significant growth in the use of multimedia for training. Macromedia has been leading the way with the introduction of such technologies as streaming Shockwave for Authorware, which was the first product to allow training applications to be streamed across intranets. Our customers are already delivering hybrid CD-ROM/Internet applications and streaming training applications across the Web. As more companies establish intranets, Web delivery will increase in importance.

What is the value of multimedia to training?

Interactive multimedia has been shown to be significantly more effective in training people than static, text-based, or classroom-based instruction. The key element is the interactivity. Interactivity and simulations improve comprehension and retention of material. Whether delivered on CD-ROM or over an intranet, interactive multimedia training applications can be delivered when employees need the training most and where it's most convenient for them, at their desktops or in their offices.

Authoring tools also allow trainers to incorporate testing mechanisms in their applications. They track a student's progress and offer more challenging material accordingly. Interactive multimedia is cost-effective and safe. Simulation offers the safest training option for new equipment or potentially hazardous processes.

Where is the multimedia industry headed? What new technologies do you see in the future that will help multimedia?

The Web is a very exciting development, allowing for cost-effective, timely, global delivery of interactive multimedia training applications. The Web also represents a treasure chest of interesting content. Trainers can incorporate live Internet links into their applications to provide the most compelling and freshest content available. We're also seeing exciting developments in collaboration technologies, such as shared whiteboards and chat; technologies that enable live, event-oriented training "broadcast" over a network simultaneously to a virtual classroom of distant learners; technologies facilitating instructor-led training in virtual classrooms; and streaming video.

Many new technologies are focusing on compression and delivery of media over the Web, making it easier and faster to deliver content.

Detail some next-wave training projects. How will new technologies change the face of multimedia training?

Some of the most creative things are the types of interactivity developers are incorporating into their training applications. Using Authorware, some developers are borrowing or adapting techniques used by game developers to solicit feedback to track students' progress. This is particularly useful in skills training and testing.

People are also increasingly leveraging their existing CBT assets and delivering them across intranets. We expect an increase in virtual classroom environments, and the incorporation of chat and instructor-led training into Web-based training applications.

What about delivery methods such as the Internet, intranets, CD-ROMs, DVD, satellite, and video? What's the most popular? Which will die?

Along with CD-ROM delivery, LAN-based training is also popular. We expect a surge in Internet-intranet delivery of training, but really don't see the other methods of delivery dying out. IP multicasting is something significant on the horizon.

Jim Buckley, CEO
CBT Systems
Menlo Park, California
800.387.0932

Company profile: A leader in the design and development of interactive education software for information technology professionals and business users.

How is technology changing the way training is delivered?

Streaming technology lets text, graphics, and audio be delivered over the Internet or a LAN. It is critical to enabling organizations to use CBT training companywide.

We invested in a company called Street Technologies. It offers us decompression and compression technologies. To deliver audio, video, graphics, and so forth, you need the ability to compress very large files and move them rapidly.

The second movement that I see on the horizon is the emergence of Java as a programming language. Java allows us [and other companies] to develop across platforms. Right now, I think of Java as a giant diesel train just leaving the station. It's strong and powerful, but not going very fast. As we get to the end of the year, it will pick up speed. There is tremendous interest in the information services community to look at, understand, and, in some sense, adopt Java.

"In general, the multimedia industry is headed for greater growth. Multimedia developers are publishers and engineers for a new medium. They integrate all of the independent forms of communication into single, dynamic pieces. In some cases, it's an art. In other cases, entertainment; in still others, business solutions. Growth should continue in different directions—be it consumer or professional, entertainment or business. The factors that will affect growth and the behavior of multimedia will be computing power, speed (particularly on the Internet), level of interactivity, and connectivity—the influence and speed of the Internet."

—Christian Dietrich
sales, marketing, and
account manager
Muffin-Head Productions,
New York

SPEAKING MULTIMEDIA

Here is a sampling from Peter G.W. Keen's *Business Multimedia Explained* (Harvard Business School Press, 1997) that will help demystify some multimedia terms.

Bandwidth. The fundamental measure of the carrying capacity of a telecommunications link. It is often referred to as a "digital pipe." The wider the pipe, the more information can flow through it. Technically, bandwidth is the range of usable frequencies of an electronic signal, but it is more generally discussed in terms of bits per second.

Cache memory. A high-speed hardware memory store that supplements a computer's larger main memory. It acts as an intermediate storage area for such items as data or program instructions that are needed often enough so that moving them constantly from a hard disk slows performance but not used often enough to justify keeping them in the main memory—the system's most limited resource.

CD-ROM. Compact-disc-read-only-memory storage is one of the foundations of multimedia. Available for about a decade, it is only since late 1993 that CD-ROM drives have become a standard feature on PCs. Of all new PCs sold, 70 percent include a CD-ROM drive.

Codec. A coder-decoder that processes nondigital data to convert it to and from digital form, and to compress and uncompress it. Codec is the computer equivalent of a modem. It converts a sound-wave signal, such as the spoken voice, or a more complex video signal, such as that produced by a camera in a videoconferencing room, to digital bit form to transmit it.

Data compression. The technique of reducing the data needed to code information in digital form by analyzing and stripping out redundant elements or summarizing items in a way that lets them be reconstituted later.

Desktop video. The capture, editing, and playback of what we see routinely in the nondigital world of television and film. It is the enabling element of multimedia in two ways: Its cost and quality define the practical limit of widespread application of multimedia tools. And it is by far the most processor-intensive component.

Frame. A single complete display on a screen or video camera. Flicker-free, full-motion video is generated by changing frames at a typical rate of 30 frames per second.

HotJava. An Internet browser that runs applications written in the Java programming language and also accesses the home pages that are the core of the World Wide Web.

Mike Yonker, CEO
Infocus
Wilsonville, Oregon
800.294.6400

Company profile: A world leader in powerful, easy-to-use multimedia projection products and presentation services. Founded in 1986 and publicly held.

Will intranets be more important than the Internet to deliver training, or the other way around?

Both will be important. For company-sensitive training, an intranet is the medium of choice. For example, we've developed a Net projector that will become a server on the Internet or an intranet. It will be able to recognize different types of browsers. That will all be possible about 1998.

What new technologies will be visible in a year or two?

Video compression will make it possible to move information much more efficiently. For example, if I try to do a PowerPoint presentation with video, sound, and graphics over the wire today, it takes forever. With compression technology, you can send a 25-megahertz file in a matter of minutes. That means easier, faster, and more seamless movement of video and data over pipelines.

Any advice for trainers?

A lot of people are lulled into thinking that all they need is the technology and their problems will get fixed. That's a recipe for disaster—a very fast disaster. Companies need to focus on the human side—helping people understand that data and change can be their greatest allies. Most people and companies fall drastically short in focusing on those principles. So, if you're spending $10 on training, spend $8 on the people side and $2 on the technology. Once you get the people side in place, they will readily accept the tools.

Steve Bradley, president
Gartner Group Learning
Stamford, Connecticut
203.964.0096

Company profile: A leading provider of IT research, advisory, and market research services.

How can media be used more effectively for training?

What's exciting for me is the "less is more" theory. By that I mean the effective and appropriate use of media, not just slamming [trainees] with a talking head. The Internet presents a whole new model and whole new way of doing things. But with respect to multimedia, it [also] presents a whole new set of challenges.

The real breakthroughs will be about managing the bandwidth challenge. That's really nothing new, and it won't be old for a long time. There will always be bandwidth challenges. The innovation is finding creative ways to manage bandwidth so you can use multimedia. The interesting thing is *how* to make multimedia more effective. In some ways, it has been overused. The bottom line is that you'll be successful to the extent that you can find out how to use 30 seconds of killer video, instead of four hours of video. Bandwidth limitations, in a way, will force all of us who want to use multimedia to be more judicious.

Do you have advice for trainers?

Yes. Trainers need to focus on skills management—having the right skills in the right place and the time to make people productive, plus using technology to manage skills. Half the battle is knowing what you need and where you need it. That means the ability to assess people, understand what skills they have, and what they need. Then, it's a matter of getting people the right skills on time.

The second part of that is finding creative ways to bring the right training to the right person in the right time frame. That is an issue of balance.

Andy Huffman, CEO
Aimtech
Nashua, New Hampshire
800.289.2884

Company profile: Develops and markets software tools used to create business multimedia applications and applets delivered by CD-ROM, networks, and the Internet. The company targets three primary market segments: employee development, electronic commerce, and interactive marketing and customer service.

Are CD-ROMs dying out?

It will probably be quite a while before it gets to that point. There will be CD-ROMs even when [most] people can deliver content on the Web. People will use less "heavy" multimedia so that they can use the Web as the delivery vehicle. The benefits of delivering on the Web are great enough that people are willing to use less media or lighter-weight media. Some developers will do the hybrid thing, in which the heavy-weight stuff is on CD-ROM.

What are some emerging applications?

One is CMI, computer-managed instruction. That software lets you manage and track [trainee] information from a server. The trend is towards more server-based management of CBT material.

The second application trend is what I call "collaborative learning." In other words, distance learning over the Internet. You'll soon see more and more companies using that technology. The great thing about distance learning collaboration is that it doesn't threaten [instructors]; it assists in the learning process.

An important development for us is Jamba, a visual authoring tool for creating Java applets and applications. It came about as we were realizing that our whole technology needed to support the Net. [Jamba] enables Internet developers, creative professionals, and Webmasters to create interactive, media-rich Java applets without programming or scripting.

"CD-ROM is mortal, which means that it's not actively dying now. With each passing month and year, it will become less the medium of choice; the medium of choice will be the Internet. CD-ROMs will be around for a long time. They are still terrific for delivering 'fat media'— audio and video files. Instructional designers need to learn how to design for self-instruction, whether that's old-style CBT, multimedia CD-ROM, or Web-based training. If it's going to be delivered by computer, it's a different instructional medium. There are different guidelines for computer or self-instruction, and there are different practices in terms of user interface."

—**Brandon Hall, editor and publisher**

Multimedia and Internet Training Newsletter

Sunnyvale, California

Art Hyde, vice president of product development
ExecuTrain Multimedia
Alpharetta, Georgia
770.667.7700

Company profile: ExecuTrain is a leader in information technology training. It is also recognized as the only training company in the industry to offer a seamless cross-delivery learning platform for both instructor-led and multimedia training.

How will technology change the face of multimedia training?

I don't think that a single technology will change the face of multimedia training in a dramatic fashion. However, the combination of several developing technologies will have a significant impact. For instance, Web-based training will address several business management issues related to employee training, including ease of deployment, centralization of tracking and progress reporting, training on demand, training in the form that [trainees] prefer, and lower cost of delivery.

Benefits of WBT to a trainee will occur when performance-based simulation becomes a standard feature of courseware. The best way to build skills and job competency is to have a [trainee] perform the necessary skills during a training session. Simulations, not "watch while I show you how to do it" or "click where I show you where to click" training segments, enable competency. Real-time, interactive 3-D graphics (available in the near future) will make simulations even more powerful and realistic.

What advice do you have for T&D readers involved in multimedia training projects?

In order to build truly effective multimedia training products, you must combine the efforts of content experts, instructional designers, and software developers.

That collaboration is a must, whether the resources are all internal or result from some type of partnership or work alliance. Both [approaches] have their positives and negatives. It is difficult to locate and compensate the required talent within the confines of a single organization. Companies that can do that generate greater profits on their own than via a partnership. Partnerships can be difficult to manage because the parties don't necessarily share common goals, even though they can benefit from the success of a collaboration.

Sacha Cohen *is former technology editor of* Training & Development *magazine.*

THE ELUSIVE FUTURE OF LEARNING TECHNOLOGIES
By George M. Piskurich, President, GMP Associates

Although it is tempting to try to make predictions about the future of learning technologies, it is likely that most predictions will turn out to be incorrect. I can still recall when most practitioners believed that video was too expensive to produce and that reel-to-reel tapes were too cumbersome to use. I can even remember when only scientists had computers, when the "Internet" was a device used for fishing, and when only a handful of people used the term "performance technology," and they couldn't agree on what it meant. New technologies will make existing technologies obsolete, while changes in the profession will vastly alter the way we think about and use technology. With these limitations in mind, I'll risk wading into the murky water of predictions and provide my best guess of where we might be going.

Possibly the most critical factor for the future of learning technologies is the profession's migration from training to human performance improvement (HPI). This movement has been gathering momentum for some time now and is on the verge of rearranging many of our thought processes, but its effect will be felt greatly in the practice of learning technologies. Within the context of improving human performance, the learning technologist should no longer be put in the situation of being asked to develop training for a technology that someone wants to try out. Having the available technology overshadow the learning needs has been detrimental to implementing learning technologies.

The flowering of HPI will also produce a far greater reliance on the use of electronic performance support systems (EPSS). These technology-based systems, in particular technology-based training, will take the place of some traditional training programs. Technology-based training is primarily used for teaching technical skills, which is also the area where EPSS will be most concentrated. Many learning technology practitioners will find themselves moving from developing training programs to developing EPSS.

This emphasis on HPI will also open doors for practitioners of learning technology to become HPI specialists. One of the most critical aspects of HPI is the performance analysis. Successful learning technologists have been using performance analysis for many years. They understand the importance of using performance analysis to choose the best intervention and identify the key steps in implementing the inter-

vention. They also emphasize the need for proper evaluation techniques to determine the success of their product. In other words, they are already performance technologists, or at the very least performance analysts. Therefore, they are prime candidates to join HPI teams.

Although I have mentioned a "learning technologist" several times, it is likely that a team of experts will handle the process of implementing and maintaining learning technology systems. The technologies have become too complex for any one individual to be able to "do it all." Learning technology is becoming a team process with designers, subject matter experts, programmers, writers, visual artists, videographers, and many others fields of expertise working together to create a learning program. Although I don't believe that the days of the corporate training department are numbered, there will probably be an increased need to partner with external service providers. Even the largest company will find it cost prohibitive to support an internal department where so many varied skills are needed. Outsourcing will provide high quality, low cost, and extremely fast service.

From the other side of the people equation, I believe the need for technology-based learning itself will expand exponentially as future generations come of age. These future employees will have grown up using computers to learn and using the Internet to find information on whatever strikes their learning fancy. I bought my 12-year-old nephew his first computer when he was eight, and my three-year-old nephew got his first one this Christmas. People with these types of educational resources are becoming truly self-directed learners and are absolutely at home with technology. They will not be effective or efficient learners in traditional learning scenarios. For them, technology-based learning will be the rule, not the exception, and we will be required to meet their need.

As for the technology itself, the Web will clearly continue to revolutionize our lives. Although it had a rocky start, most great technologies require a period of evolution and social acceptance. Bandwidth and other problems will be solved, formats will be standardized, and before too long every company with more than one employee will have some type of Web-based training process in place. Although it won't take the place of all classroom training or all OJT or mentoring, it will become an integral delivery system for training. Web-based training will provide immediate disbursement of training in a just-in-time scenario and timely revisions, two solutions to problems that have vexed both technology-based and nontechnology-based learning practitioners for generations.

These new technologies will also integrate training delivery with training administration to the point that the distinction between the two will become invisible. This will finally allow training professionals to collect accurate data for evaluation purposes at a relatively low cost. This type of integrated system is already being implemented in some places. I am presently involved in a project where trainee data, down to the "which questions were missed on a quiz" level, will be automatically uploaded through the Web to a site that anyone in the company with the proper authorization can access.

The next frontier for learning technologies will be virtual reality. Virtual reality will manifest itself in a number of different uses, from three-dimensional models on a computer screen to the total immersion experience that can be created through the use of tactile gear. The visual and auditory aspects of virtual reality already exist, while more advanced tactile technologies are on the horizon. Voice recognition is in its infancy, but when it is combined with tactile gear, the ultimate EPSS system can be created. This EPSS system could have a troubleshooting program that allows the user to describe the problem, then gives an exact simulation of how to fix the problem. Again, all of these ideas return to the notion that EPSS and HPI will continue to merge together.

Many HRD practitioners have been accused, sometimes rightfully, of touting each new technology as a replacement for all currently existing learning methodologies. Perhaps we've grown wise enough to know that such claims have rarely been correct. Learning technologies cannot stand effectively on their own. They must be integrated with other systems and processes such as classroom instruction, on-the-job learning, or management interventions. Finally, people throughout the organization must support the use of technologies for learning purposes. Although we can't really guess what technologies will emerge in the future, it is important to remember that the technologies themselves are only one part of the equation.

LEARNING TECHNOLOGIES AS WE ENTER THE 21ST CENTURY
By Angus Reynolds, Professor, Southern Illinois University

But we cannot live the afternoon of life according to the programme of life's morning; for what was great in the morning will be little at evening, and what in the morning was true will at evening become a lie.—Carl Jung

Although Carl Jung was not intentionally writing about learning technology, the famous psychiatrist hit the nail on the head! Things change. Our field has witnessed big changes in the decades since World War II, and we will see more change in the next century.

We in the learning technology field are lucky to be able to see change coming so clearly. The evolution of learning technology can be foreseen by *anyone* in the field. It will be a natural progression. The major developments will be written about long before they become available. If we take the time to read our industry's periodicals, we will not be surprised when new technology comes to the market. We will be able to forecast how changes can be used in our own organizations or situations.

Advances in system capabilities are always followed by progress in what we can use the technology to accomplish. The astronauts went to the moon with computing power that is 1/10,000th of what we may have on our desks.

Today we can perform highly sophisticated simulations on the desktop and deliver multimedia learning activities over the Internet. These capabilities make a big difference in the training that we can offer. Better yet, the trend continues.

One mistake is to believe the hype that seems to accompany all new technology. Another is to cling to any contemporary technology as the be-all and end-all of HRD. We should use the new technology for what it's worth and be ready for what we will be able to do better, faster, and cheaper tomorrow. Internet working has changed the way we communicate and do business. Learning technology is now even more closely related to common business technology. Those who recognize this fundamental shift and master the new technology will be ready for tomorrow.

Juan Sebastián del Cano completed the first voyage around the world in 1522, taking over two years. In 1873, Jules Verne wrote the fictional *Around the World in Eighty Days*. About 100 years later, anyone could fly around the world on a routine commercial Pan American Airways flight in approximately four days. In 1961 Yuri Alekseyevich Gagarin circumnavigated the world alone in the spacecraft Vostok 1, in under two hours! When we employ new technologies in the next century, the world of learning will be a little smaller. If we make the best use of evolving learning technologies, it will also be better!

EPSS: IS IT REALLY A LEARNING TECHNOLOGY?
By Kim Ruyle, President and CEO, Plus Delta Performance Inc.

Is EPSS a learning technology? If so, is it more properly classified as an instructional method or a presentation method? The answers to these questions depend on the instructional intent that the designers ascribed to the application.

An electronic performance support system (EPSS) is a comprehensive, computer-based job aid that provides just-in-time, just-what's-needed assistance to performers on the job. An EPSS typically includes several or all of the following:

◆ database of job-required information organized to facilitate rapid access and optimize clarity
◆ calculators and wizards that simplify and automate procedures
◆ decision-support modules that provide intelligent assistance with problem solving
◆ embedded tutorials and simulations that provide instruction in work-related concepts and procedures.

Just as a hand tool leverages physical capabilities, an EPSS leverages cognitive capabilities. It can provide adaptive support for a full range of cognitive tasks. In effect, an EPSS makes performers smarter, but generally for only as long as they are using the application. EPSS technology is only a learning technology to the extent that it causes learning (an internalized, long-term ability to do something new).

Although it's almost heretical to admit in a community of trainers, designers of EPSS applications don't usually care if learning takes place. The focus is on performance, not learning. When learning is important, designers opt for instructional interventions that can be thought of as events. There is a beginning and an end to the instructional experience. By the conclusion of the event, the learner has internalized the ability to do something new. Job aids, on the other hand, do not have a beginning or an end, and they do not cause an internal change in the performer (notice the contrast between learner and performer). Job aids are external to the person.

EPSS is difficult to classify as a learning technology because instructional intent is latent or nonexistent except for embedded tutorials and simulations. At the point at which instructional modules are accessed, an EPSS is essentially functioning as a standard instructional method, typically as multimedia CBT or simulation. For EPSS developers, perhaps it's more important to have a model to guide decisions about instructional intent than it is to have a classification scheme.

APPENDIX B NATIONAL HRD EXECUTIVE SURVEY ON LEARNING TECHNOLOGIES
By Mark Van Buren

Learning Technologies
1997 Second Quarter Survey Report

Special Note to the Reader:
This study was completed before the classification system for learning technologies was created. Therefore the article does not use the same terms and distinctions found in the rest of this book.

Introduction
Since the field of HRD has long relied on technology to deliver its services, this issue of the National HRD Executive Survey focused on the use of "information technology," including some of the newest delivery methods such as the Internet and groupware. Since many of these technologies have the potential to promote a shift from training in the classroom to learning on the job, they are increasingly referred to as "learning technologies." The survey gathered information around the following key questions:

◆ How important are new learning technologies?
◆ To what extent is the field of HRD using learning technologies to deliver its services **today**?
◆ To what extent will the field of HRD use learning technologies to deliver its services **tomorrow**?
◆ How are decisions about the use of learning technologies made?
◆ What are the primary challenges and hurdles surrounding the use of learning technologies?

To summarize the results below, the survey panel members are of the widespread belief that learning technologies are not only important today, but that collectively their potential to serve as a delivery method in the future is tremendous. However, panelists also identified several hurdles that HRD professionals must overcome if learning technologies are to reach their full potential, particularly the need to keep pace with the rate of change and to be able to assess when and where learning technologies will be most effective.

Results[5]

I. Importance of Learning Technologies
When asked to indicate the importance of investing in learning technologies, nearly 70 percent of HRD executives indicated that such investments are "very important" (see figure 1A). Taken together with those who indicated that they are "somewhat important," nearly 96 percent see learning technologies as a key investment.

It is also clear that most HRD executives (over 80 percent) think that the top executives of their organizations believe investing in learning technologies

---

5 *See table 7 for description of respondents.*

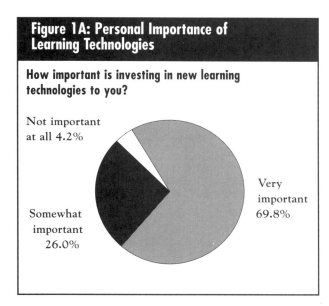

Figure 1A: Personal Importance of Learning Technologies

How important is investing in new learning technologies to you?

Not important at all 4.2%
Somewhat important 26.0%
Very important 69.8%

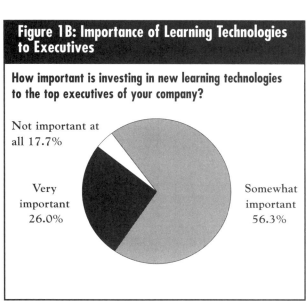

Figure 1B: Importance of Learning Technologies to Executives

How important is investing in new learning technologies to the top executives of your company?

Not important at all 17.7%
Very important 26.0%
Somewhat important 56.3%

to be important too (see figure 1B). However, they reported that top executives are more likely to see investing in learning technologies as "somewhat important" rather than "very important."

One way in which the lower priority that top executives place on learning technologies manifests itself is in the allocation of budgeted dollars for learning technologies. Survey respondents reported that typically their organizations set aside only one percent (median; mean = 6.6 percent) of their entire 1997 budget for designing, developing, implementing, and purchasing new learning technologies. Of these funds, organizations usually budget about 25 percent

(median; mean = 36.7 percent) for purchasing products or services from outside providers, further evidence of the growing reliance on outsourcing.

HRD executives also reported that they are no strangers to the use of information technology in their own work. Almost all respondents (95 percent) indicated that they use a personal computer every day, and over 80 percent reported using electronic mail every day (see figure 2). A distant third, but still surprising, is the Internet and World Wide Web, which 25.5 percent of respondents said they use every day. Few respondents reported using electronic performance support systems (EPSS) or authoring tools regularly.

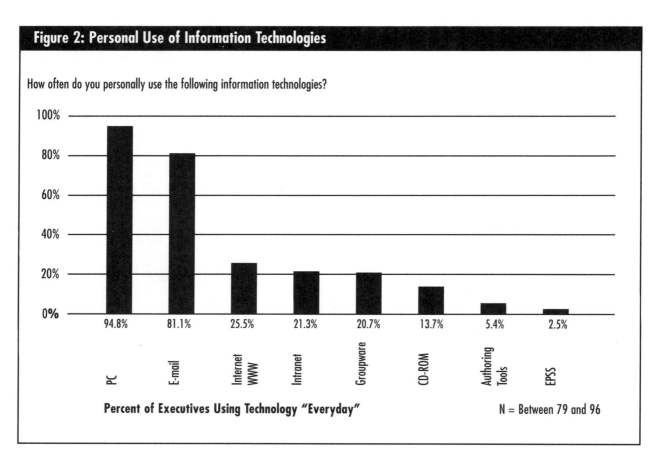

Figure 2: Personal Use of Information Technologies

How often do you personally use the following information technologies?

Technology	Percent
PC	94.8%
E-mail	81.1%
Internet WWW	25.5%
Intranet	21.3%
Groupware	20.7%
CD-ROM	13.7%
Authoring Tools	5.4%
EPSS	2.5%

Percent of Executives Using Technology "Everyday"

N = Between 79 and 96

II. Use of Learning Technologies

If any single finding stands out from the survey, it is the clear trend toward the greater use of learning technologies. Figure 3 illustrates the distribution of training time delivered by learning technologies versus instructor-led and other methods for 1996, 1997, and 2000. In 1996 respondents reported that on average, 10 percent of their organizations' training time was delivered by new learning technologies. Respondents expected the amount of training time delivered by new learning technologies to grow by an average of 67 percent in 1997.

This sizable increase, however, pales in comparison to their projection that the figure will more than triple by the year 2000. By that point, panelists project that an average of 35 percent of all training time will be delivered by learning technologies. Training delivery via instructor-led methods is expected to experience a corresponding decrease from 80 to 55 percent of all training time. Other methods of delivery should remain constant throughout the period.

Researchers also asked respondents to indicate which learning technologies they are using or will be using to deliver training. Table 1 summarizes the diffusion of learning technologies across organizations represented in the National HRD Executive Survey for the same three points in time, ranked by the extent of their use in 1996. The results reveal that

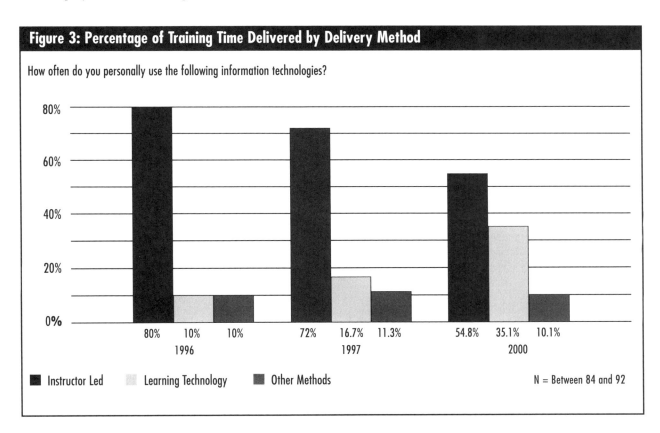

Figure 3: Percentage of Training Time Delivered by Delivery Method

How often do you personally use the following information technologies?

80% 10% 10% | 72% 16.7% 11.3% | 54.8% 35.1% 10.1%
1996 | 1997 | 2000

■ Instructor Led   ■ Learning Technology   ■ Other Methods   N = Between 84 and 92

the top three choices for delivering training in 1996—CBT on disk or hard drive, video teleconferencing, and CBT on CD-ROM or CD-i—are likely to remain the top choices in 1997 as well.

However, by 2000, the most common learning technologies are expected to change dramatically. Respondents project that large percentages of organizations will use distributive technologies capable of combining text, video, and audio digitally-intranets, multi-media on local or wide area networks, and the Internet or World Wide Web. A comparison of the 1996 and 1997 results reveals that this trend is already underway. The use of intranets is expected to more than triple (from 14 percent to 45 percent) and the use of the Internet and Web is expected to grow from 27 percent to 48 percent. Substantially more respondents also expect to use local or wide area networks-whether CBT or multimedia-this year than last.

Table 1: Percent of Companies Using Learning Technologies by Year (N = 96)

Learning Technology	Used in 1996	Will be Used in 1997	Plan to Use by the Year 2000
CBT: disk/hard drive	55.2	63.5	36.5
Video Teleconferencing	53.1	56.3	42.7
CBT: CD-ROM/CD-i	42.7	54.2	32.3
Interactive Television/Video (Including Satellite)	37.5	42.7	41.7
Multimedia: CD-ROM/CD-i	29.2	37.5	40.6
Internet/World Wide Web	27.1	47.9	45.8
CBT: LAN/WAN	21.9	41.7	42.7
Computer Teleconferencing	14.6	22.9	40.6
Intranet	13.5	44.8	57.3
Multimedia: LAN/WAN	12.5	24.0	46.9
EPSS	4.2	13.5	24.0
Virtual Reality/Electronic Simulation	1.0	2.1	20.8

III. Decisions About Learning Technologies

The above results suggest that many organizations are facing the need to make critical decisions around the use of learning technologies. Researchers asked respondents what aspects of introducing and managing learning technologies they are responsible for today. Table 2 summarizes the degree to which HRD departments versus other groups are responsible for these activities. The activities are listed in order of HRD involvement, from highest to lowest, using a scale of 0 (not involved) to 2 (primarily responsible).

Table 2: Level of Involvement in Learning Technology Activities (N Varies by Activity)

Activity	HR/Training Department	IS Department	Other Department	Outside Provider
Designing the Training Contents	1.90	0.71	0.83	0.69
Identifying Potential HRD-Related Technology Applications	1.89	1.04	0.83	0.36
Maintaining/Upgrading the Training Contents	1.82	0.99	0.58	0.52
Implementing/Rolling Out the Technology	1.51	1.45	0.84	0.34
Maintaining/Upgrading the Learning Technology	1.45	1.52	0.51	0.38
Selecting Potential Technology Vendors	1.40	1.47	0.68	0.25
Financing the Purchasing of the Technology	1.26	1.35	1.22	0.02
Financing the Design and Development of the Technology	1.25	1.44	1.12	0.16
Developing Your Company's Strategic Information Technology Plan	0.83	1.83	0.82	0.37
Designing the Hardware/Physical Components	0.67	1.84	0.52	0.69
Developing the Hardware/Physical Components	0.62	1.80	0.42	0.82

Not surprisingly, the top three responsibilities of HRD departments regarding learning technologies involve identifying potential applications and designing and maintaining their training content. More surprising was the finding that HRD and information systems (IS) departments tend to be equally involved in implementing learning technologies and selecting the technology vendors. Both activities require that HRD practitioners be fairly technologically informed and conversant—skills that should prove increasingly necessary for delivering HRD services.

IS departments, on the other hand, tend to take responsibility for developing and designing the hardware, and putting together the strategic information technology plan. Other departments, most likely finance, tend to be most involved in financing the purchasing as well as the design and development of learning technologies. The involvement of outside providers appears to be relatively low at this time,

with their highest level of involvement being developing the hardware.

Table 3 provides additional information about how organizations identify potential HRD-related applications for technology. The table lists the criteria organizations use to decide whether to implement a learning technology or use another delivery method. The criteria are ranked from highest to lowest using a scale of 1 (least important) to 8 (most important).

Respondents report that the most important criterion is the type of skills to be learned. For instance, how complex are the skills, how frequently do the skills change, and are they hard or soft skills? Short- and long-term costs of the learning technology application and characteristics of the learners ranked closely behind the type of skills to be learned. Table 3 also reveals that these criteria were most likely to be listed among the three most important. The availability of qualified design, delivery, and support personnel ranked as the least important criterion.

Table 3: Criteria for Implementing Learning Technologies (N = 90)

Rank	Criteria	Mean Rating	Percent Top 3
1	Type of skills to be learned (for example, level of complexity, how frequently the skills change)	4.98	60.4
2	Costs (short-term and long-term)	4.74	60.4
3	Learner characteristics (for example, number of people, current skill level, geographic dispersion)	4.12	46.2
4	Time (e.g., how quickly and how frequently material needs to be delivered)	3.98	36.7
5	Evidence of the learning technology's effectiveness	3.78	45.6
6	Current and future technological capacity and flexibility	3.42	34.4
7	Support capacity (availability of qualified design, delivery, and support personnel)	3.08	22.0
8	Other	1.40	20.0

Evidence of the effectiveness of a given learning technology ranked somewhere in the middle of the list of criteria above. Table 4 suggests the reason why. When asked about the types of information respondents have the most difficult time finding, the top choice was information on how to choose among learning technologies. Moreover, six respondents

specifically wrote in information on "effectiveness" as one of their top three choices. Respondents also ranked information on how to implement new learning technologies and what companies or HRD executives are doing as difficult to find. Information on leading vendors appears to be the most easily located.

As shown in table 5, HRD executives draw on HRD magazines as the primary source of information on learning technologies. The most frequently mentioned examples were *Training & Development* (15) and *Training* (15) magazines. Rounding out the top three sources of information, but further behind, were HRD conferences and events and other HRD professionals. The Internet and Web are the sources that HRD executives mentioned they rely upon the least.

IV. Future Challenges

Finally, researchers asked respondents what they consider to be the most important challenges between now and the year 2000 in using learning technologies. The challenges are listed in table 6, ranked in importance from highest to lowest using a scale of 1 (least important) to 10 (most important).

Table 4: Difficulty of Finding Information on Learning Technology (N = 85)

Rank	Type of Information	Mean Rating	Percent Top 3
1	Information on how to choose among learning technologies	5.20	68.2
2	Information on how to implement new learning technologies	4.60	56.5
3	Information on what other companies or HRD executives are doing	4.44	35.3
4	Information on the technological skills HRD professionals will need in the future	3.60	32.9
5	Information geared toward executive-level HRD professionals	3.49	35.7
6	Information on the very latest technological developments	3.44	32.1
7	Information on the leading vendors	3.14	27.4
8	Other information	2.33	33.3

Table 5: Sources of Information on Learning Technology (N = 86)

Rank	Source	Mean Rating	Percent Top 3
1	HRD Magazines	4.40	74.1
2	HRD Conferences/Events	3.65	60.2
3	Other HRD Executives or Practitioners	3.38	44.7
4	Other Parts of Your Company	3.35	47.7
5	Non-HRD Magazines	3.24	44.2
6	Other Sources	2.58	41.9
7	Internet/World Wide Web	2.03	19.2

Nearly 55 percent of respondents reported that keeping pace with the rate of change looms as their biggest challenge over the next few years. With the length of time it takes to develop and implement new technologies, the rapid rate at which new technologies are introduced often means that learning technologies are no longer state of the art by the time they are fully operational. This suggests another reason for the trend illustrated in table 1 toward the use of learning technologies that are flexible, can be easily customized, and are quickly deployed without a large change in technology infrastructure.

The next two most important challenges—assessing effectiveness and determining fruitful applications—add additional urgency to the call for information on effectiveness and knowing when and where to implement learning technologies discussed with table 4. The magnitude of the expenditure outlays often required for introducing new learning technologies requires that HRD executives be able to justify those expenditures and demonstrate their potential value and benefits to the organization. Unfortunately meaningful assessments of effectiveness and value are difficult to conduct at this time.

Table 6: Future Challenges in Using Learning Technologies (N = 93)

Rank	Challenges	Mean Rating	Percent Top 3
1	Keeping pace with the rate of change	5.92	54.3
2	Assessing the effectiveness of new learning technologies	5.55	39.6
3	Knowing when and where to apply new learning technologies	5.54	41.8
4	Integrating existing technologies with new learning technologies	5.49	35.2
5	Getting top management buy-in	5.02	45.2
6	Delivering existing courses/training using new learning technologies	4.49	18.7
7	Developing new courses/training for new learning technologies	4.41	22.8
8	Encouraging employees to use new learning technologies	4.30	23.9
9	Finding HRD professionals knowledgeable about new learning technologies	3.76	18.5
10	Other	3.42	29.2

One additional future challenge mentioned frequently under "Other" challenges was obtaining sufficient resources—particularly funding, but also time and personnel—to use new technologies. This finding provides additional support for the finding reported in table 3 about the importance of cost as a criterion in determining whether to implement new learning technologies.

About This Survey

Researchers sent the 1997 National HRD Executive Survey on Learning Technologies to the 275 members of the survey panel. Invitations to join the panel were also extended to an additional 700 HRD executives drawn from ASTD's membership and a random sample of 1,000 human resource managers in the U.S. These results were based on the 96 responses we received. Of these, 78 came from existing panel members for a panel response rate of 28 percent. Table 7 describes the characteristics of the respondents.

Table 7: Respondent Characteristics

Industry (N = 86)	Percentage
Agriculture, Construction	3.5
Manufacturing	22.1
Transportation, Communication, Public Utilities	10.5
Trade	5.8
Finance, Insurance, Real Estate	22.1
Health	18.6
Services	9.3
Public/Government	8.1

Profit Status (N=94)	Percentage
For-Profit	64.9
Not-for-Profit/Nonprofit	35.1

Table 7: Respondent Characteristics (continued)

Sales (N = 86)	Percentage
$1 million to $49 million	6.8
$50 million to $249 million	1.7
$250 million to $999 million	25.4
$1 billion or more	66.1

Function (N = 86)	Percentage
Strategic Human Resources	2.4
Training	51.2
Performance Improvement	10.7
Organizational Development	10.7
General Human Resources	15.5
Other	9.5

Establishment Size:	950 Employees (Median)
Firm Size:	5,500 Employees (Median)

TRAINING INDUSTRY TRENDS 1997

BY LAURIE J. BASSI, SCOTT CHENEY, AND MARK VAN BUREN

An annual look at trends, by the research department of the
American Society for Training & Development.

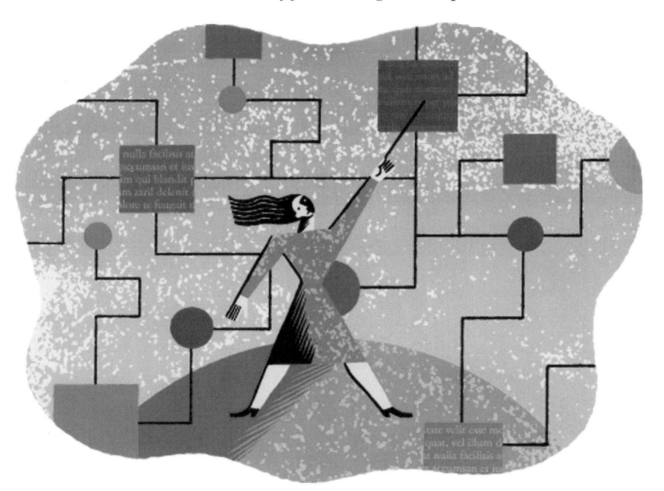

For centuries, the "technology" for trans-
ferring skills and knowledge has changed little: one human being teaching another. Generations of classroom trainers have deployed the time-honored "chalk and talk" approach. Only the overhead projector loomed on the horizon of a training landscape devoid of technology. Now, that landscape is awash with a torrent of new technologies,

creating almost limitless possibilities for heightened learning.

These days, a variety of electronic media can facilitate the transfer of knowledge and skills. That represents both a challenge and an opportunity for professionals who specialize in workplace learning and performance. Technological innovation is constantly and pervasively altering the way in which work is done. That, in turn, has immediate consequences for the demands on specialists in workplace learning and performance improvement. The rapid pace of change requires that workplace learning occur on a just-in-time, just-what's-needed, and just-where-it's-needed basis. The same technological forces behind the restructuring of work are also enabling (and requiring) the workplace learning community to create more flexible and responsive learning and performance solutions.

At the same time, the increasing openness, democratization, and globalization of the world economy have made it clear that to compete effectively, businesses must be the best in the world at what they do. That has caused corporations to hone their core competencies to be world-class.

At firms operating in developed economies, core competencies are being defined in the context of knowledge-based work. In a world where technology and financial capital move across national boundaries with speed and ease, employees are the main, if not only, source of competitive advantage. In high-wage, developed countries, employees must be able to produce value-added, knowledge-based products and services. The often-heard CEO's mantra that "people are our most important asset" has been drowned out many times by the roar of downsizing and other policies that belie the importance of human capital. But there are signs that is changing. Emerging interest in knowledge management and intellectual capital suggests that firms are, in fact, attempting to manage and leverage knowledge (and the human beings who possess it) more effectively.

The importance of learning, and learning quickly, to a company's long-run viability means that workplace learning is becoming a significant strategy. The bar is set high in terms of the skills required of professionals in workplace learning and the standards of accountability to which they are held.

"The Top 10 Trends" in the November 1996 issue of *Training & Development* identified these trends:

1. Skill requirements will continue to increase in response to rapid technological change. More than half of the new jobs created between 1984 and 2005 will require some education beyond high school (*Workforce 2000: Work and Workers for the 21st Century*, 1987). Since 1984, the percentage of workers who use a computer in their jobs has risen from 25 to 46 percent (*Level of Access and Use of Computers: 1984, 1989, and 1993*, U.S. Bureau of the Census, 1993).

2. The American workforce will be significantly more educated and diverse. Despite the challenge of hiring skilled workers, Americans are staying in school longer. The percentage of women, older workers, and Asian and Hispanic workers will continue to increase through 2005 (*Employment Outlook: 1994-2005 Job Quality and Other Aspects of Projected Employment Growth*, U.S. Department of Labor, 1995).

3. Corporate restructuring will continue to reshape the business environment. Downsizings, more small businesses, a lack of job security, and low employee morale will continue to affect the type of training and how it's delivered.

4. The size and composition of training departments will change dramatically; 58 percent of large U.S. corporations have downsized their HRD departments (*Rethinking Human Resources: A Research Report*, the Conference Board, New York, 1995).

5. Advances in technology will revolutionize training delivery. Developments in hardware, computer networking, multimedia software, and videoconferencing have tremendous potential for multiple-site delivery and bringing training closer to people's work sites.

6. Training departments will find new ways to deliver services. To cope with the demand for quality instruction, they are creating structures to support networks of internal and external providers, such as consultants and community colleges.

7. There will be more focus on performance improvement. In a survey of training professionals at ASTD's 1996 International Conference, 89 percent "strongly agreed" or "agreed" that a shift from training to performance improvement is a top trend. Training professionals now borrow from such areas as organizational development, industrial and organizational psychology, and strategic human resources to provide performance improvement interventions.

8. Integrated high-performance work systems will proliferate. Training departments—like all business units—are being forced to re-examine their role and focus more on measurable results. The new emphasis will be on creating systems that align the separate efforts of functions, departments, and people.

9. Companies will transform into learning organizations. In a 1995 ASTD National HRD Executive Survey, 94 percent of respondents said they thought it was important to build a learning organization; only 9 percent said their companies weren't moving in that direction. In a learning organization, training is integral to work—a by-product of work rather than something done in isolation. The role of training professionals in learning organizations is to find ways to capture and share knowledge systematically as work occurs and changes.

10. Organizational emphasis on human performance management will accelerate. More organizations are using multilevel performance-management elements, such as gainsharing and team rewards. Many are tying performance management to business goals, such as expressing goals in terms of cycle time, quality metrics, or customer satisfaction. They're also reviewing employees' performance in the context of meeting such goals. And they're taking an interest in job analysis, evaluation, competency modeling, skill standards, and testing.

ASTD believes that trends 4, 5, 6, and 7 will be especially influential in shaping the landscape of workplace learning and performance improvement. This article provides more detail

DISTINCTIONS AND DEFINITIONS OF LEARNING TECHNOLOGIES

The term *learning technologies* creates some confusion. It combines two separate and distinct phenomena—a presentation method (such as interactive multimedia, videoconferencing, and EPSS) with a distribution or delivery method (such as CD-ROMs, the Web, and audiotapes). For example, interactive multimedia is a presentation method that can be delivered through such delivery methods as CD-ROM, LAN (local area network), and WAN (wide area network). In addition, various instructional methods (separate and distinct from presentation methods and delivery methods) are available for any particular learning technology. Instructional methods include lectures, games, group discussion, and role play—delivered electronically or through such traditional means as classroom training. Electronic learning technologies are a subset of all learning technologies.

Though the following list of learning technologies isn't exhaustive, we offer the following distinctions and definitions:

Learning Technologies. The use of electronic technologies to deliver information and facilitate the development of skills and knowledge.

Distinctions

▸ **instructional methods.** How information is taught to learners. Such approaches include lectures, literature, games, demonstrations, expert panels, case studies, exercises, group discussion, simulations, and role play.

▸ **presentation methods.** How information is presented to learners. Such methods include electronic text, computer-based training, interactive TV, multimedia, teleconferencing, online help, groupware, virtual reality, audio, video, and electronic performance support systems.

▸ **distribution methods.** How information is delivered to learners. Such methods include satellite and cable TV; LAN/WAN networks; computer disks; the Web (the Internet, intranets, and extranets); CD-ROMs; email and voicemail; simulators; audiotapes and videotapes; and telephone.

Definitions

Presentation methods.

▸ **electronic text.** The dissemination of text via electronic means.

▸ **CBT.** A general term used to describe any learning event that uses computers as the primary distribution method; typically used to refer primarily to text-based, computer-delivered training.

▸ **multimedia.** A computer application that uses any combination of text, graphics, audio, animation and/or full-motion video. Interactive multimedia enables the user to control various aspects of the training, such as content sequence.

▸ **interactive TV.** One-way video combined with two-way audio or other electronic response system.

▸ **teleconferencing.** The instantaneous exchange of audio, video, or text between two or more individuals or groups at two or more locations.

▸ **online help.** A computer application that provides online assistance to employees.

▸ **groupware.** An integrated computer application that supports collaborative group efforts through the sharing of calendars for project management and scheduling, collective document preparation, email handling, shared database access, electronic meetings, and other activities.

▸ **virtual reality.** A computer application that provides an interactive, immersive, and three-dimensional learning experience through fully functional, realistic models.

▸ **audio.** One-way delivery of live or recorded sound.

▸ **video.** One-way delivery of live or recorded full-motion pictures.

▸ **electronic performance support system (EPSS).** An integrated computer application that uses any combination of expert systems, hypertext, embedded animation, and/or hypermedia to help a user perform a task in real time quickly and with a minimum of support by other people.

Distribution methods.

▸ **cable TV.** The transmission of television signals via cable technology.

▸ **CD-ROM.** A format and system for recording, storing, and retrieving electronic information on a compact disc that is read using an optical drive.

▸ **electronic mail (email).** The exchange of messages through computers.

▸ **extranet.** A collaborative network that uses Internet technology to link organizations with their suppliers, customers, or other organizations that share common goals or information.

▸ **Internet.** A loose confederation of computer networks around the world that are connected through several primary networks.

▸ **intranet.** A general term describing any network contained within an organization; used to refer primarily to networks that use Internet technology.

▸ **local area network (LAN).** A network of computers sharing the resources of a single processor or server within a relatively small geographic area.

▸ **satellite TV.** The transmission of television signals via satellites.

▸ **simulator.** A device or system that replicates or imitates a real device or system.

▸ **voicemail.** An automated, electronic telephone answering system.

▸ **wide area network (WAN).** A network of computers sharing the resources of one or more processors or servers over a relatively large geographic area.

▸ **World Wide Web.** All of the resources and users on the Internet using the Hypertext Transport Protocol (HTTP), a set of rules for exchanging files.

We'd like your input on these definitions and distinctions. Send comments to panderson@astd.org.

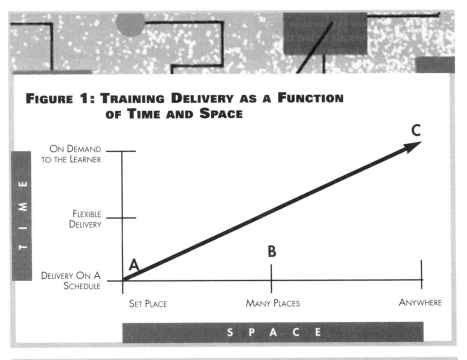

FIGURE 1: TRAINING DELIVERY AS A FUNCTION OF TIME AND SPACE

TIME
- ON DEMAND TO THE LEARNER
- FLEXIBLE DELIVERY
- DELIVERY ON A SCHEDULE

A   B   C

SPACE
SET PLACE   MANY PLACES   ANYWHERE

TABLE 1: USE OF ELECTRONIC LEARNING TECHNOLOGIES

LEARNING TECHNOLOGY	PERCENTAGE USING TECHNOLOGY IN 1996	PERCENTAGE EXPECTING TO USE TECHNOLOGY IN 1997	RANK IN THE YEAR 2000
CBT: disc/hard drive	55.2	63.5	9
Video-teleconferencing	53.1	56.3	5
CBT: CD-ROM/CD-i	42.7	54.2	10
Interactive television/video (including satellite)	37.5	42.7	6
Multimedia: CD-ROM/CD-i	29.2	37.5	7
Internet/Web	27.1	47.9	3
CBT: LAN/WAN	21.9	41.7	4
Computer teleconferencing	14.6	22.9	8
Intranet	13.5	44.8	1
Multimedia: LAN/WAN	12.5	24.0	2
EPSS	4.2	13.5	11
Virtual reality/electronic simulation	1.0	2.1	12

(SOURCE: ASTD's NATIONAL HRD EXECUTIVE SURVEY, 1997)

paper and pencil. To others, it means only technologies presented or delivered electronically. (See the box, Distinctions and Definitions of Learning Technologies.) A unifying attribute of learning technologies is that they seek to enhance the flexibility of learning options via electronic means.

In Figure 1, traditional classroom training is represented by point A. Most electronic learning technologies inhabit the spaces to the north and east of point A. Teleconferencing, for example, lets training take place at multiple locations but requires a designated training time (point B). Because of their flexibility, learning technologies enable learners to escape from the fixed, inflexible time-space demands of a classroom. C represents the point at which a technology can enable learning to occur anytime, anyplace. For people with the appropriate hardware, that technology includes intranets and the Internet.

Until recently, companies have been exploring the use of the Internet and intranets cautiously. But as technology continues to improve their efficiency, the Internet and intranets will increasingly be used to deliver training. Many businesses already have internal webs.

The Information Technology Association of America estimates that HRD and training departments are heavy users of intranets (*HR Magazine,* January 1997). Industries that deliver training via the Internet or intranets doubled their activity between 1996 and the first quarter of 1997 (*Business Wire,* February 1997). External sources that develop company training systems via electronic learning technologies have grown in conjunction with the recent corporate interest in outsourcing multiple aspects of training.

For example, CBT Systems in Menlo Park, California, markets to large companies training courses delivered over their intranets. Other suppliers, such as Logical Operations Interactive and Microsoft Online Learning Institute, have also established niches in the intranet market (*Computer Shopper,* February 1997).

Another new Internet option is the Business Channel, offered jointly by The Williams Companies and Public Broadcasting Service. The Business Channel provides interactive training

on the key aspects of these trends: learning technologies (trend 5), outsourcing (a component of trends 4 and 6), and performance measurements (a component of trend 7).

The use of electronic learning technologies to deliver information and facilitate the development of skills and knowledge will revolutionize learning. But despite increasing use of the term *learning technologies,* it doesn't have a universally accepted definition. To some people, it means any technology used to facilitate learning, including

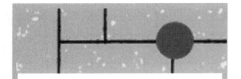

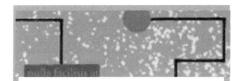

BENEFITS AT A GLANCE

Here are some potential benefits of electronic learning technologies for training delivery.

▶ **greater cost-effectiveness.** More people trained more often, reduced cost, flexibility to add participants without additional cost.

▶ **increased quality of instruction.** Access to remote experts, more program choices; multiple opportunities for instructor and participant interaction.

▶ **self-paced, individualized.** Participants learn at levels comfortable for them, at times convenient to them.

▶ **fewer resource requirements.** Classrooms, trainers, and other classroom-related resources aren't needed.

▶ **decentralized training.** Learning can occur anytime, anywhere, anyplace.

▶ **tireless delivery.** Trainers can get tired, but technology is always available for consistent delivery.

(Source: *Selecting and Implementing Computer-Based Training*, National Workforce Collaborative, 1997)

neously to share information and communicate worldwide. That makes delivery more consistent on an as-needed basis. The greatest drawback is the lack of reliable interactive, multimedia capabilities (*Knowledge Inc.*, February 1997). But as advances in technology conquer that problem, intranet and Internet use will increase. New developments will remove some of the technical roadblocks, such as bandwidth limitations, and create opportunities for more dynamic intranet training systems, including video and animation.

Ultimately, the Internet and corporate intranets will be the major mechanisms for interactive, multimedia training delivered anywhere and on-demand. Until then, when highly interactive training is needed, other learning technologies such as video-conferencing and traditional training are more effective (*Technical & Skills Training*, January 1997).

A clear distinction between the Internet and intranets is the speed with which training applications can be delivered. Many delivered via the Internet are relatively slow. Intranets can be much faster because they have an open standard for delivery instead of being tied to one supplier's system. Because of an intranet's capability to streamline communication and enhance performance, the intranet market will exceed the Internet market in 1999 by a ratio of two to one, according to Zona Research.

After the initial investment in the required technological resources, intranets are usually cheaper than other distance learning tools because they can be maintained and updated easily and quickly. They don't require printed materials or CD-ROMs. And users can access training as needed in real time. But as technology improves the Internet's speed and security, the distinction between it and intranets will blur, according to Ovum, a consulting firm in Burlington, Massachusetts.

Many companies are already taking advantage of training via the Internet and intranets. Ernst & Young uses its intranet to distribute training materials to employees. Strategic Interactive, a software firm, is developing a training system to give employees of auto companies access to job training on the Internet from any location at any time of day (*APA Monitor*, March

CHOOSING FROM THE ALTERNATIVES

The wide variety of electronic learning technologies makes it hard to know which is the most cost-effective and beneficial for conveying information, knowledge, and skills. The critical factors to consider are the content, audience, expected learning gains, and costs—fixed and marginal.

More research is needed on how to determine a particular learning technology's potential benefits, but the total cost can be calculated, albeit with some difficulty. The fixed expenses of development can be high, but the marginal expenses (per additional learner) tend to be low. Consequently, the total cost varies with the size of the audience. And even though the cost of a particular learning technology may be prohibitive, a technological breakthrough (which might be right around the corner) could make it more feasible financially.

Generally, the smaller and more geographically concentrated a particular audience, the more likely traditional classroom training will be the most cost-effective. Conversely, the larger and more geographically dispersed the audience, the more likely some form of electronic learning technology will be most cost-effective. In some cases, a combination (such as classroom training with an electronic technology) may be best.

over the Internet, with on-demand training to subscribing organizations ("PBS Heads to the Desktop," by S. Bradley, *Meetings and Conventions*, January 30, 1997).

Although use of the Internet and intranets to deliver training is not yet widespread, it's expected to jump dramatically in the next three years. (See Table 1 on page 121.) Eighty-one percent of the companies that are members of ASTD's Benchmarking Forum anticipate an increase in using the Internet for internal training.

A major benefit of training delivery via the Internet or an intranet is that different computers and different operating systems can be used simulta-

1997). The Gartner Group of Stamford, Connecticut, created the Internet Learning Center to provide interactive courses on information technology.

A critical question concerning learning technologies is their cost-effectiveness compared with tra-

USING LEARNING TECHNOLOGIES

In the April 1997 National HRD Executive Survey, the 275 panel members discussed trends regarding learning technologies. The survey sheds light on the extent to which organizations are using or expect to use electronic learning technologies as delivery systems. It also identifies the roles of HRD professionals in using learning technologies and the challenges they can expect to face.

A primary finding was confirmation of the significance of learning technologies. The results reveal that investing in learning technologies is of widespread importance to both HRD executives (92 percent) and top executives (82 percent). But respondents attach different degrees of importance to such investments. Seventy percent of the HRD executives said that learning technology investments are "very important," compared with slightly less than 18 percent of the top executives.

Another finding was a greater use of learning technologies. Respondents reported that, on average, 10 percent of their organizations' training time in 1996 was delivered by new learning technologies. They expected that figure to rise by 67 percent in 1997 and triple by 2000. They predicted that by then, 35 percent of all training will be delivered by learning technologies. They expect instructor-led training to decrease from 80 to 55 percent.

A close look at the use of individual learning technologies shows that the top three choices for delivering training in 1996—CBT on disk or hard drive, video-teleconferencing, and CBT on CD-ROM—are likely to remain the top choices in 1997. But by 2000, the most common learning technologies are expected to change dramatically. Respondents predicted that many organizations will use distributive technologies capable of combining text, video, and audio digitally—such as intranets, multimedia on local or wide-area networks, and the Internet or Web.

A comparison of the 1996 and 1997 figures reveals that this trend is already in gear. The use of intranets is expected to more than triple (from 14 to 45 percent); the use of the Internet and Web is expected to soar from 27 to 48 percent. Substantially more respondents expect to use LANs and WANs (either with CBT or multimedia) this year than last.

The survey also indicates that HRD professionals are already taking primary responsibility for certain aspects of introducing and managing learning technologies. Their tasks include identifying potential applications, designing and maintaining training content, and implementing and maintaining the learning technologies. The last two require HRD practitioners to be technologically informed and conversant. Developing and designing the hardware are still the province of information systems.

Identifying potential HRD-related applications for technology can be a daunting task, without knowing what criteria to use. HRD executives say that the most important criteria center around the type of skills to be learned—how complex they are, how frequently they change, and whether they are hard or soft skills. Next in importance are the costs, short- and long-term, of a learning technology application. Next in importance are the characteristics of the learners—how many, their geographic dispersion, their current skill levels, and so forth.

Nearly 55 percent of the HRD execs said that keeping pace with the rate of change looms as their biggest challenge. Considering the time it takes to develop and implement new learning technologies and the rapid rate at which they're introduced, they're no longer state-of-the-art by the time they're fully operational. That targets a trend towards the use of flexible learning technologies that can be customized easily and deployed quickly, without a major change in the technology infrastructure.

Two additional challenges are how to assess the effectiveness of learning technologies and how to determine their useful applications. The costly initial outlay of such technologies requires HRD people to be able to justify the expense and demonstrate the potential value.

Overall, the surveyed HRD executives think that the potential of learning technologies to serve as a delivery method is tremendous. However, there are some critical hurdles to overcome: the need to keep pace with the rapid rate of change and the need to assess when and where learning technologies will be most effective.

ditional training approaches. In an era of budget cuts and downsizings, the evidence that electronic learning technologies can reduce training time and costs (and train more people more often) is causing great interest. Unfortunately, there's little solid research comparing the cost-effectiveness of traditional versus electronic approaches. Nevertheless, here is some evidence that electronic learning technologies can be highly cost-effective.

▶ A consortium, GATE (Government Alliance for Training and Education), reports that training time and costs have been reduced significantly by distance learning at the U.S. Department of Energy and Federal Aviation Administration.

▶ The U.S. Coast Guard has used multimedia for several training initiatives, resulting in significant annual savings due to less need for instructors (*Training,* February 1997).

▶ At the AT&T Center for Excellence in Distance Learning, videoconferencing and other distance learning resulted in significant cost savings ("It's Time To Change the Way We Train!" by A.

Chute, H. Starin, and D. Thompson, 1996, http://www.lucent.com/cedl/dlnewslt.html).

◗ A 1992 study by Pennsylvania State University suggests that employee retention during training via distance learning is equal or superior to classroom instruction. Another study shows that interactive video-based instruction achieved a 25 to 50 percent higher retention rate than classroom instruction (*Multimedia and Videodisc Monitor,* March 1992). More evidence shows that the quality of learning is higher with either interactive CBT training (*Interactive Video-Based Training-On-Demand Over Multimedia Networks,* August 1995) or other self-directed, computer-based training (*Wall Street Journal,* January 3, 1996) than traditional instruction.

◗ The speedy rate of training delivery is a clear advantage of most electronic learning technologies. Case studies show that self-paced, multimedia training can take 20 to 80 percent less time than instructor-led training, due to a tighter instructional design and learners' option to bypass content already mastered (*Training & Development,* February 1996). A survey of more than 100 companies shows that multimedia training can reduce learning time by 50 percent, compared with classroom training.

◗ Companies such as Apple Computer, Andersen Worldwide, and Storage Technology report less training time with multimedia. Storage Technology technicians who were once required to travel to a central location for four to 10 days of training now receive training through a localized multimedia system, saving $1.5 million over a three-year period (*Journal of Interactive Instruction Development,* Winter 1996).

◗ Some studies suggest no significant difference between new and traditional training approaches in terms of learning and employee satisfaction (http://www.usdla.org/dl.html, 1997).

The box, Benefits at a Glance, on page 122 shows the potential advantages of electronic learning technologies.

Although there is a dearth of systematic, high-quality information on cost, employers generally think that electronic learning technologies are more expensive than class-

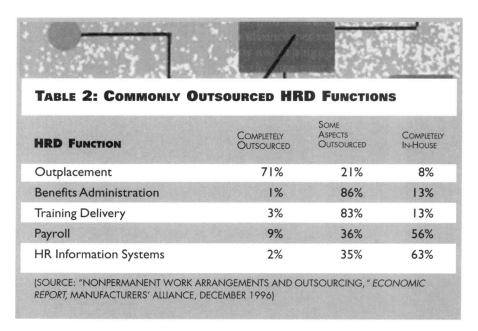

TABLE 2: COMMONLY OUTSOURCED HRD FUNCTIONS

HRD Function	Completely Outsourced	Some Aspects Outsourced	Completely In-House
Outplacement	71%	21%	8%
Benefits Administration	1%	86%	13%
Training Delivery	3%	83%	13%
Payroll	9%	36%	56%
HR Information Systems	2%	35%	63%

(SOURCE: "NONPERMANENT WORK ARRANGEMENTS AND OUTSOURCING," *ECONOMIC REPORT,* MANUFACTURERS' ALLIANCE, DECEMBER 1996)

room training. A 1996 survey by the Seybold Group found that 78 percent of respondents considered cost to be an obstacle to using multimedia CBT courseware (*The ASTD Training Data Book,* by Laurie Bassi, Anne Gallagher, and Ed Schroer, ASTD, 1996). A 1996 survey found that the median number of person-hours required to develop one hour of CBT is about 200 (*Computer-Based Training Report,* by Floyd Kemske, SB Communications, Hingham, Massachusetts). At a rate of $50 per hour, the average cost of developing an hour of CBT would be $10,000.

It's unclear, however, to what extent the high fixed costs of electronic learning technologies are offset by their greater cost-effectiveness in the long-run. A study by the AMR Training and Consulting Group estimates a high return-on-investment from electronic learning technologies (particularly for multimedia-based training) ranging from 100 to 400 percent. But some estimates on ROI for traditional training are even higher. Unfortunately, no available sources directly compare the return-on-investment of electronic learning technologies with the ROI of traditional training.

Outsourcing

More focus on core competencies and cost containment has led many companies to rely on outsourcing—

called the "growth industry of the nineties." Outsourcing is becoming an essential management tool. In 1996, more than 90 percent of organizations outsourced at least one activity (Michael F. Corbett & Associates, Poughkeepsie, New York, http://www.corbettassociates.com).

According to a recent survey conducted by the Outsourcing Institute, more than half of all organizations increased their use of outsourcing in 1996. U.S. companies spent about $100 billion outsourcing various business functions. By 2001, that figure is expected to surge to $318 billion, according to Corbett & Associates. In an April 1996 issue of *Business Week,* Tom Peters called outsourcing "the most sweeping trend to hit management since reengineering."

Though many companies consider employees' knowledge, skills, and abilities critical to success, few view training as a core competency. Consequently, the training function has become a prime candidate for outsourcing. A recent survey by the Manufacturers' Alliance shows that HRD functions, including training, are most often cited as areas in which outsourcing will increase. Table 2 shows that though outsourcing all training delivery is rare (3 percent of firms), most companies (83 percent) outsource at least some training. Data from the Outsourcing Institute is consistent with that finding. In 1996, more HRD activities (84 percent) were outsourced than any other functions. Logistics and information technology were outsourced at 52 and 51 percent. The average outsourcing of other functions was 30 percent.

Countervailing forces alert us to consider the outsourcing trend carefully. The need for greater corporate agility demands just-what's-needed solutions, which require a closer link between training and performance. In a 1995 ASTD National HRD Executive Survey on performance support, 84 percent of the respondents said there would be a closer link between training and performance by 2000. In the July 1997 National HRD Executive Survey, respondents said the most significant HRD trend in the next three years will be a shift from providing training to improving performance. Interestingly, respondents did not identify outsourcing as a significant trend.

Integrating training with performance improvement has implications for outsourcing. By keeping performance-related training in-house and outsourcing such training as computer skills, employers can use resources more effectively. For example, Corning outsources individual learning courses while maintaining courses focused on institutional learning and performance in-house. Rethinking training as part of performance management helps tie training effectiveness more directly to specific business goals. That can make outsourcing ineffective beyond a certain point.

Dow Chemical's outsourcing approach appears to have struck a balance between countervailing forces. It is based on a distinction between strategic and tactical training. Though Dow recently outsourced all tactical aspects of training (scheduling, materials control, and delivery), in its U.S. locations, it kept the strategic aspects (design, development, integration, and evaluation) in-house. That enables employees to focus on managing goals and the impact of training and performance improvement on the company.

Defining the term. *Outsourcing* is an umbrella term. In its broadest sense, it's synonymous with external and clearly distinguished from in-house. In the context of training, outsourcing can describe an array of training services or a few. At the extreme, outsourcing involves using external consultants to manage all aspects of training—from design and development to delivery and evaluation.

DuPont is perhaps the most widely cited example of that form of outsourcing, sometimes referred to as *insourcing.* Insourcing requires the merging of resources both inside and outside of an organization for unique training solutions. Specifically, external providers collaborate with employees to create a new entity responsible for everything from daily training operations to long-term planning. DuPont claims the approach has been successful because of internal expertise and external objectivity (*Boston Globe,* January 7, 1997).

Frequently, employers enlist the services of external providers for specific aspects of training, including bringing consultants in-house to conduct training or to train internal trainers so that training is an internal function. For example, Digital Equipment Corporation doesn't consider training to be a core competency, so 80 percent of its training, including most design and delivery, is outsourced. Only strategic planning and technical training (considered vital to Digital's business goals) are internal activities. Digital's outsourcing exists primarily through partnerships with local training consultants, specific suppliers such as Microsoft, and global training houses.

Among the members of ASTD's Benchmarking Forum, three companies outsource at least 40 percent of design, development, instruction, administration, and technical support; three others maintain almost all of those functions in-house. In contrast, forum member Aetna has undergone a dramatic reorganization in which it eliminated its training group and let go hundreds of trainers. Some outsourcing replaced internal staff, and more outsourcing is anticipated.

Most companies fall in the middle of the outsourcing continuum. They rely neither on internal staff or external providers completely. Still, most have done more outsourcing in the past year and will continue. A 1995

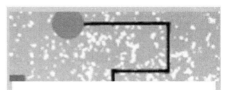

TOP 10 TRENDS

Here are the top 10 HRD trends, according to respondents to the July 1997 National HRD Executive Survey.

Currently

1. Computer skills training
2. Teamwork training
3. Shift from training to performance
4. Decision-making and problem-solving training
5. Rapid development and deployment of training
6. Systems-thinking training
7. Demonstrating training outcomes
8. Measuring performance outcomes
9. Shift from training to learning
10. Making a business case for training interventions

Next three years

1. Shift from training to performance
2. Computer skills training
3. Shift from training to learning
4. Virtual organizations
5. Demonstrating training outcomes
6. Measuring performance outcomes
7. Delivering training to meet specific needs
8. Emphasis on knowledge management
9. Rapid development and deployment of training
10. Teamwork training

survey by Dataquest Worldwide Services shows that almost two-thirds of the respondents used outside suppliers to develop customized courseware; more than 40 percent used external sources for needs assessment. Many of those companies anticipate more need for outside training services over the next two years.

A recent survey by the U.S. Bureau of Labor Statistics indicates that small firms (fewer than 500 employees) spend more than 50 percent of their training budgets on outside suppliers (*Expenditures on Employer-Provided Training,* by Laurie Bassi, ASTD, July 1996). The National Association of Manufacturers says that small employers, who tend to use community colleges and other low-priced training providers, will use such services more often (*Training,* December 1995).

An expanding market. Data from a sample of U.S. firms (1994 EQW National Employer Survey) indicates that employers are using a wide variety of external training providers. As outsourcing grows, an increase in the size, number, and type of providers is likely. Such independent providers as community and technical colleges, universities, profit-oriented learning and development centers, and private industry associations are discovering new business opportunities in outsourcing.

Though most of the external training market began with a focus on specific products, such as training for a new piece of machinery, it has recently and quickly expanded to include training services. According to Dataquest, external suppliers increasingly provide customized training geared to employers' needs.

The short life cycles of technology products, compounded by the greater complexity of many job roles, are expected to heighten the demand for external information-technology education providers and other training providers. For example, New Horizons Computer Learning Centers, one of the largest computer training businesses in the world, plans to open 170 new training facilities worldwide within the next three years (*Adult Assessment Forum,* Winter 1996).

Also on the rise is classroom training at community and technical colleges and in the corporate education departments of four-year colleges and universities. Although community colleges have offered training programs to local businesses for decades, more are jumping at the opportunity to form partnerships with companies. The American Association of Community Colleges estimates that the num-

ber of community colleges actively seeking to provide training to companies has jumped from about 50 percent in 1990 to 90 percent (*Training,* December 1995).

Technical institutes, such as those in Wisconsin's technical college system, continue to provide training for employers. In a recent survey by Wisconsin Manufacturers and Commerce,

> ■ *Partnerships between two-year schools and corporations point to contract training arrangements becoming a significant presence in the training supplier market* ■

a statewide business association, the technical college system was listed as the most important external training resource for in-state employers; 58 percent report using them to meet specialized training needs. Fifty-three percent report using other outside providers such as consultants; 24 percent rely on four-year colleges or graduate schools. Several four-year colleges and universities have established separate corporate education divisions that provide training on a contract basis.

Such programs are being developed and adapted to target corporations by addressing their specific needs, ranging from basic computer training to strategic solutions. Such institutions as Gateway Community College in Phoenix have found a niche in the supplier market on training and workforce development for small businesses. Most of the programs have a common focus on the particular needs of employers, including needs assessment, design, development, and instruction. Maricopa Community College, also in Phoenix, developed a specialized training curriculum to support Motorola's semi-

conductor-manufacturing process (*Training,* December 1995). Mesa Community College, one of the 10 colleges that make up the Maricopa system, established a joint curriculum committee with Motorola to design courses (*Technical & Skills Training,* August/September 1992). Terra Community College in Ohio and Chippewa Valley Technical College in Wisconsin offer general training support services, such as course registration and employee testing. To meet employers' needs, many local colleges have expanded their educational offerings to new areas—such as quality, ISO 9000, and sales training. Rio Salado Community College created two new associate degrees—in airline operations and customer service—for America West Airlines and American Express (*Human Resource Executive,* February 1996).

The training offered by community colleges, technical institutes, and corporate education departments differs from the academic and career development tracks of four-year colleges and universities, primarily because of its emphasis on developing workplace skills. Some community colleges reinforce the commitment to providing workplace-relevant training by guaranteeing the skills of their graduates to employers and by offering additional training at no charge for dissatisfied employers. A focus on workplace-relevant training is also reflected in the schools' common practice of hiring local professionals to help design and teach many of the contract courses. Although full-time faculty are generally involved in developing and delivering the courses, the schools think it's important to draw on the experience of seasoned professionals to ensure that material is up-to-date, practical, and useful. Such experts are often chosen from the businesses seeking the training.

Unlike four-year colleges and universities, community and technical colleges and corporate education departments usually establish a location separate from their campuses. At Delta Community College in Saginaw, Michigan, corporate contract training is a distinct entity from its other two-year education programs. Delta began providing auto-maintenance training programs for General Motors more than 10 years ago. Since then, the college has established Delta Corporate Services, a separate function offering both local and global training services to organizations. Its use varies from the implementation of one-time, specific programs to comprehensive services. At one firm's Michigan facilities, DCS is responsible for training management, support, and delivery. Although training is conducted at the firm's worksite, DCS delivers all of it. Boston University's Center for Corporate Education is also a separate entity, with its own 200-acre campus and administration. Teachers at the center are called trainers instead of professors, and each has practical experience in the corporate world.

Local colleges and corporate education departments have tended to establish formal partnerships or alliances with businesses. Norton Manufacturing, an Ohio-based crankshaft maker, developed an alliance with Terra Community College and several state agencies to provide employee training and testing. Similarly, Union Pacific Railroad partnered with Salt Lake City Community College to provide training to its 35,000 employees (*Human Resource Executive,* February 1996). Employees spend two weeks on campus and then participate in six months of self-study, with support from the college's instructors. By entering into such partnerships with businesses, the community colleges, technical colleges, and continuing education departments forge a unique and participative role as education providers interested not only in developing the private sector workforce, but also in tackling employer-specific challenges. Companies still tend to turn to four-year colleges and universities for management and executive training, while local colleges tend to gear their programs to technical and rank-and-file employees.

Although the services provided by some of the schools mentioned may be more expansive than the services offered by most local colleges, partnerships between two-year schools and corporations point to contract training arrangements becoming a significant presence in the training supplier market.

Another important outside source of training are trade and professional associations. There's little research on the role of such associations as suppliers. Yet, employers consistently cite them as an important resource. A scan of the literature on national trade associations in a few large industries (retail, hotel, health care, and pharmaceuticals) suggests that trade associations play a role in the delivery of industry-specific training, although often through field offices at the local level. For example, the American Pharmaceutical Association delivers APhA-developed education programs in conjunction with various state-level pharmaceutical associations.

Trade and professional associations also serve as facilitators or clearinghouses of information on training providers. In addition to providing its own seminars, the American Dental Association maintains a list of more than 300 dental education providers. Some associations act as standard-setters by helping estab-

> ■ *The trend towards greater outsourcing of training is not only apparent by the behavior of employers and colleges but also by the interest of investors* ■

lish skill standards or by designing and developing courseware marketed to employers. The American Hotel and Motel Association's Educational Institute provides a variety of materials for home study and hotel-based classrooms. The institute also offers certification programs in hotel administration, food and beverage services, sales, and operations, as well as distance learning courses and on-site consulting services in training management. The National Retail Federation is developing employee

certification programs, using skill standards set by retailers in the industry.

Labor unions are also involved in providing training, though usually as an advisor or a partner in curriculum development rather than delivery. Since 1986, the Communications Workers of America, International Brotherhood of Electrical Workers, and AT&T have managed worker training at AT&T through the AT&T Alliance, an independent not-for-profit organization run jointly by the unions and management (*Labor's Key Role in Workplace Training,* by M. Roberts and R. Wozniak, AFL-CIO, 1994). The Alliance offers such services as career planning and assessment, basic skills training, occupational training, personal finance planning, exam preparation, and stress management.

The trend towards greater outsourcing of training is not only apparent by the behavior of employers and colleges but also by the interest of investors. Specialized training firms, such as Computer Learning Centers, have become publicly traded firms in an effort to capitalize on and fuel their rapid expansion. Taking advantage of opportunities in the corporate world, CLC recently spun off a new division, Advantec Institute, that offers customized computer classes geared towards employers' needs. Based on the positive response so far (and the realization that the demand for such services is greater than the supply), CLC anticipates continuing its expansion into the domain of corporate training, particularly in providing customized packages.

Other training and development companies are emerging in corporate markets and capturing the interest of Wall Street. CBT Systems, Learning Tree International, National Education Corporation, and Westcott Communications, among others, have received heightened attention from business investors after recently making public stock offerings.

Smith Barney advises its clients that a well-balanced portfolio should include investments in education and training providers. It segments its coverage of that sector into these groups: education management organizations,

TO OUTSOURCE OR NOT OUTSOURCE? THAT IS THE QUESTION

In collaboration with ASTD staff, a group of representatives from ASTD's Benchmarking Forum is developing an outsourcing decision-making tool that will be described in an upcoming issue of *Training & Development*. First, the group defined *outsourcing* as "using noncompany resources to provide some or all of the training, learning, and performance-improvement products and services needed to support a company's strategic direction."

Here are some questions to ask when deciding whether to outsource an initiative.

▶ What's the business case?
▶ Are internal support systems required for the initiative?
▶ Can we provide a wide-enough variety of products and services?
▶ What capabilities do we have in-house? What is our skill mix?
▶ How often will we have to update?
▶ Is a stable supplier available?

Regarding the audience and time constraints,

▶ Who are our target participants?
▶ What is their geographic dispersion?
▶ Do we have peaks and valleys in our needs?
▶ When is the training required?
▶ What is the time period for preparation?
▶ Is there time to reskill?

Regarding cost and value,

▶ What are the actual systems costs of maintaining the initiative internally, compared with outsourcing it?
▶ What are the cost constraints?
▶ What is the payback period?
▶ What is the global value-added aspect? Can it be achieved with outsourcing?

Regarding strategic focus,

▶ How does our culture affect this decision?
▶ Does it make sense from a systems perspective?
▶ Can outsourcing decisions be integrated into a systemic solution?
▶ How would outsourcing affect the ability to maintain control of strategic issues?
▶ What is the role of changing technology?

Here are some reasons to outsource and their relevant questions.

To gain access to world-class capabilities.

▶ Do state-of-the-art skills exist internally or externally?
▶ What would it take to get them? (the time, staff, facilities, skills, values, and so forth)
▶ How reliable is the outside expertise?
▶ Can it be done faster? More effectively?

To increase the operational efficiency of the training and learning function.

▶ Are other organizations performing the same operations at a better value or cost than we are?

To improve training's contribution to core initiatives and strategies.

▶ Where can the training department and its staff add value?
▶ Do we lack internal expertise and staff?
▶ Do we have enough staff to perform the initiative in time?
▶ Is the audience so small or large that it warrants outsourcing? Or do the benefits warrant internal expertise?
▶ How often is the desired expertise needed?

To specialize training, add flexibility, improve timeliness, and reduce costs.

▶ Can we build flexibility with existing resources?
▶ Do we have to provide training globally?
▶ Is the purpose to move from fixed to variable costs or to reduce costs?
▶ How long will payback take?
▶ How long do we have to achieve the desired results?
▶ What are the costs and benefits?

The questions of why and what to outsource can be difficult to untangle. The group determined that each of the general questions can be applied function-by-function in determining what to outsource. Such functions include administration and analysis (determining where you want to be, where you are, and what performance is needed to achieve business goals); identifying performance gaps; and projecting the benefits. Other functions include design (identifying the appropriate actions and specifications) and development (creating the performance initiative).

Additional functions are implementation; application support (transferring learning on-the-job); evaluation (measuring performance improvement); and managing the outsourcing.

The group created this goal: To design and implement cross-functional processes to facilitate successful outsourcing. The management activities of outsourcing fall into these categories: planning, communications, supplier management, and feedback and reporting. To accomplish the identified goal, it's necessary to address internal and external factors.

Internal

▶ Identify stakeholders; map their degree of support and interest. Get them on board early—philosophically and functionally.

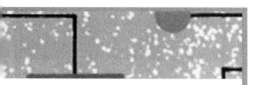

- Ensure that there's a process for aligning the proposed initiative with overall goals.
- Continue to evaluate internal resources.
- Report to management the potential business results.
- Orient internal staff to the need for, and benefits from, outsourcing.
- Teach training staff about supplier management.
- Understand the costs and the implications on the company's culture.
- Determine whether there are global implications.
- Identify legal issues, such as dual employment.
- Identify and involve key support functions, such as purchasing and communications.
- Conduct ongoing evaluation of outsourcing as a business strategy.

External
- Develop and use supplier selection and certification tools.
- Define suppliers' scope and their expectations.
- Determine whether the relationship will be teaming or contracting. If teaming, communicate the big picture to suppliers: we sink or swim together.
- Write and manage performance contracts with suppliers.
- Conduct ongoing evaluation of the suppliers.
- Determine whether your company is best-served by one, a few, or many suppliers.
- Know their corporate cultures.
- Provide ongoing feedback to suppliers regarding their performance.

training and development providers, and instructional media companies.

With regard to the last two, Smith Barney bases its advice on these big drivers:
- the trend towards outsourcing
- the evolution from a manufacturing-based to a knowledge-based economy
- the ubiquitous nature of technology
- changes in the workplace
- advances in communications technology
- the global economy.

In a presentation at ISA's annual conference in March 1997, Charles Hall, director of Smith Barney's Education Group, cited evidence that during the past two years, training and development stocks had appreciated at more than twice the rate of Standard & Poor's Industrials.

Smith Barney is not alone in being drawn to the education and training sector, made up of 5,300 for-profit firms. Montgomery Securities and Piper Jaffray have also developed education and training investment lines; others are poised to enter the market. The legendary investor Warren Buffett has taken an active interest in the for-profit training and education industry, particularly by buying FlightSafety International, considered the largest U.S. training firm. Former junk bond king Michael Milken, with a partner, invested $125 million in Knowledge Universe, a training and consulting company expected to reach $1 billion in sales by year end (*Business Week,* August 4, 1997). The actions of those savvy investors signify the growth of the training and development industry. Training stocks are selling for 30 to 50 times expected earnings, a phenomenon that also characterized the behavior of technology stocks in their boom. As training firms continue to expand and offer new tools to meet specific company demands, Wall Street's interest will surely grow.

Performance measurement
Efforts to cut costs, focus on core competencies (and outsource the rest), and use learning as a strategic source of competitive advantage all point to the need for ongoing, accurate evaluation. In a survey of more

than 1,000 training professionals at ASTD's 1996 International Conference, 93 percent said they are under increased pressure to demonstrate return-on-investment. In the July 1997 National HRD Executive Survey, the need to measure performance outcomes is high on senior practitioners' list of current and future HRD trends.

It has never been easy to isolate (credibly) training's effect from other performance improvement interventions. The reliance on electronic learning technologies (such as EPSS) will almost certainly complicate that already difficult task. Yet, in an era when learning is central to competitive advantage and all corporate functions are held to new standards of accountability, the challenge must be met head-on.

An important point often missed is the debate regarding the value of measuring training's effect, including ROI. On one side, the thinking is that what gets measured gets managed. If workplace learning initiatives aren't measured sufficiently, it's highly unlikely that they'll be well-managed. That will be particularly true as more electronic learning technologies become available and choosing among them becomes more complex. It has too-often been ignored that measurement is a component of good management and essential to continuous improvement.

With those considerations in mind, several Benchmarking Forum companies began working together in September 1996 to improve evaluation approaches. At the first meeting of the Performance Metrics Working Group, it constructed this guiding principle: "Our purpose is to use measurement as a means to promote continuous improvement in the cost and performance effectiveness of learning."

Substantial efforts are underway at many Benchmarking Forum companies to tie training more closely to business outcomes. That appears to be one fad that won't go away. Here are some buzzwords that top management continues to use and take seriously:
- shareholder value
- profitability
- efficiency
- customer satisfaction
- return-on-investment (at the corporate level)

- return-on-assets
- cycle time
- performance.

Training professionals must understand and speak that language, and be able to translate the results of their work into those concepts. Inherent in the language are metrics for linking the results of training and learning to business outcomes and strategies.

In its efforts to improve measurement and evaluation on behalf of the entire profession, the PMWG recognizes the need to provide meaningful benchmarks of training outcomes in the language spoken by senior managers and CEOs. The group also realizes that it will take time and effort to achieve that objective. Though the group's goal is to benchmark training and education outcomes at Level 4 and beyond, it knows that it's necessary to walk before running. So, it chose to concentrate its initial efforts on Levels 1 and 3. Group members agreed that Level 2 evaluation, though important for the purpose of continuous improvement, would be too difficult to implement uniformly across firms and interventions.

From work being done at several companies, it appears that Level 1 data—when thoughtfully structured, gathered, and analyzed—has a greater benefit than previously recognized. In particular, early evidence suggests that Level 1 data may have some predictive validity for the types of information desired from Level 3 and 4 evaluations. In fact, Level 1 data may have the potential to be a useful, timely, and cost-effective short-run predictor of the long-term effects of training. As a result, Level 1 data can possibly be harnessed for the purpose of the continuous improvement of training and its outcomes.

To realize the full potential of reaction data, Level 1 questions must extend beyond smile sheets. To maximize its usefulness, a Level 1 evaluation should include questions on such issues as a course's relevance regarding job requirements, timeliness, accuracy of content, and ease of registration—in other words, utility-oriented questions.

One of PMWG's intentions is to investigate fully whether and to what extent Level 1 data can indicate Level 3 measures. If such a predictive capacity exists, Level 1 data can be used to improve the likelihood that new skills and behaviors will be transferred on the job.

In early 1998, the initial work of the Performance Metrics Working Group will be published in *Training & Development,* including a core set of Level 1 and Level 3 survey questions designed to apply across firms. The core questions, which can be supplemented with questions tailored to a firm's specific needs, cover training outcomes, as well as the barriers and enablers to effective training. Though the PMWG still has much to do, its initial work will, for the first time, enable the systematic benchmarking of training outcomes. Perhaps more importantly, it will result in valuable information for generating continuous improvement.

Emerging trends

Several potentially significant emerging issues have least two factors in common: One, they result from the ongoing evolutionary needs and opportunities of doing business in the information age. Two, they're likely to have profound implications for people working in the arena of workplace learning and performance improvement.

Routine work that can be automated or exported to low-wage countries has all but disappeared in high-wage, developed nations—making it clear that the only basis for sustainable competitive advantage is through value-added, knowledge-based work. Seen in that light, it's not surprising that there is a growing interest in knowledge management in the corporate and academic communities.

At some level, knowledge management—which can be defined as the process of creating, capturing, and using knowledge to enhance organizational performance—is nothing new. All firms must manage knowledge in some way or quickly go out of business. What is new is that it's active, purposeful, and often an explicit responsibility of a senior manager—for example, the chief knowledge officer.

Although knowledge management can encompass a broad array of activities, it is associated mainly with activities that try to document and appropriate people's knowledge (codified knowledge) and disseminate that knowledge throughout an organization. Typically, such activities are conducted through a company-wide database. Knowledge management also includes activities that facilitate human exchanges through such venues as interactive software, email, and the Internet.

Examples of knowledge-appropriating activities include
- creating knowledge bases or databases in which proven solutions are shared
- compiling corporate "yellow pages" —directories of employees with specialized knowledge
- creating lists of experts to whom employees or customers can ask questions.

Examples of human exchange activities include
- establishing employee Web sites, chat rooms, and email functions to facilitate personal communication and share knowledge among employees
- using interactive software such as Groupware or online forums so that more than one person can work on a problem at the same time
- arranging and financing face-to-face meetings between people working at different locations.

From the perspective of workplace learning, there are two striking aspects of knowledge management. One, such efforts try to capture and capitalize on the informal approaches through which people learn as a by-product of doing their work. Two, such efforts appear only rarely to be tied to a company's formal mechanisms (such as training) for creating knowledge among workers.

That suggests there is an important, but unrealized, opportunity for ensuring that knowledge management initiatives are well-integrated with formal education and training. It also suggests that firms are recognizing the strategic importance of informal learning and that people responsible for workplace learning should take heed of this development.

Intellectual capital

One evidence of the intensified interest in intellectual capital is three recent books with that term in the titles.

Each book defines intellectual capital somewhat differently, but all agree on the hidden value:

- intellectual property
- know-how
- customer loyalty
- information about customers and suppliers
- processes and technology systems
- patents and trademarks
- corporate culture
- employees' competencies, skills, knowledge, and morale.

All three books say that intellectual capital has been swept under the rug of goodwill and that it's time to create, manage, measure, and leverage intellectual capital. They say that in the next millennium, "the value is not in the tangible assets but in the intangible ones." They also say that knowledge is more valuable and more powerful than natural resources, big factories, or fat bankrolls.

The books warn that double-entry bookkeeping systems (in which expenditures on education and training are recorded as costs) are the enemy of intellectual capital and that to realize fully its value, corporations need better systems for measuring intangibles. Companies need to develop better measures of the investments (such as training) they make in human capital and the value such investments produce.

According to the books' authors, such measures are important because they're needed for effective management and because they can predict future performance. Academics and other experts say that standard accounting measures fail to quantify performance. If nonfinancial measures can predict future performance, such measures can also attract financial capital to companies managing their intellectual capital wisely.

There is no "there"
The discovery of the steam engine resulted in the Industrial Revolution, which resulted in a fundamental reorganization of human economic and social activity—work and life adapted to the needs and opportunities of an industrial era rather than an agricultural era. Semiconductor-integrated circuits are the steam engines of information processing and a catalyst for another fundamental reorganization of human activity—from what was compatible with the industrial age to what is consistent with the information age.

The dawn of the information age has given rise to virtual corporations—which, according to Davidow and Malone, "to the outside observer will appear almost edgeless, with permeable and continuously changing interfaces between company, supplier, and customers. From inside, the view will be no less amorphous, with traditional offices, departments, and operating divisions constantly re-forming according to need. Job responsibilities will regularly shift, as will lines of authority—even the very definition of employee will change." Since that was written in 1992, other aspects of the inside view of a virtual organization have become apparent. In many cases, there is no "there." Instead, people work at home, in their cars, at airports, and even on beaches.

> ■ *People work at home, in their cars, at airports, and even on beaches* ■

The emergence of virtual corporations prompts mostly unanswered questions. How will employees acquire the knowledge and skills for rapidly changing responsibilities? How will we instill and maintain important aspects of corporate culture when people work in geographic isolation? How do we promote teamwork when people rarely, if ever, see each other face-to-face?

How do we deal with *disintermediation?*—a term coined by Don Tapscott in his book, *The Digital Economy.* According to Tapscott, "Middleman functions between producers and consumers are being eliminated through digital networks. Middle businesses, functions, and people need to move up the food chain to create new value or they face being disintermediated." Tapscott warns that if a company has in its midst agents, wholesalers, distributors, retailers, brokers, or middle managers, it's time to do some serious strategizing (or career planning, if you're one of them).

That advice speaks to many profitable businesses and their functions. At some level, professionals responsible for workplace learning and training have always been brokers—brokers of information. As electronic learning technologies replace traditional training, the brokerage function becomes more apparent. The task essentially becomes matching learning needs with available technologies. But as the information for making a good match becomes more readily available, the need for the brokerage function diminishes. Logically, in a digital economy, workers will have the capacity to locate and obtain exactly the training they need, thus bypassing the middleman.

Tapscott's advice to people who serve as brokers is to find ways to *re-intermediate*—a terrible term, he admits, meaning to add value. The shift from training to performance improvement represents one way to do that. ■

Laurie J. Bassi *is vice president of research,* **Scott Cheney** *is director of the Benchmarking Forum, and* **Mark Van Buren** *is senior research officer at the American Society for Training & Development, 1640 King Street, Box 1443, Alexandria, VA 22313-2043; phone 703.683.8100; fax 703.683.8103.*

The authors thank the following people who contributed to this report: Benchmarking Forum representatives Jayne Bleicher, Aetna; Sonya Fox, Corning; John White, Dow Chemical Company; and Bob Mjos, Digital Equipment Corporation. ASTD staff Phil Anderson, Katherine Dols, Patricia Galagan, Ethan Sanders, and Ed Schroer also contributed. Anne Gallagher was research assistant, and Laurie Buchannan worked on an earlier version.

Presentation Methods	Satellite TV	Cable TV	LAN/WAN	Web Internet Intranet Extranet	CD-ROM/DVD	E-Mail	Voice Mail	Tactile Gear/Simulator	Audiotape	Videotape	Telephone	Computer Disk
Audio			X	X	X		X		X		X	X
CBT			X	X	X							X
Electronic Text			X	X	X	X						X
EPSS			X	X	X							X
Groupware			X	X								X
Interactive TV	X	X										
Multimedia			X	X	X			X				X
Online Help			X	X	X							X
Teleconferencing	X	X	X	X							X	
Video	X	X	X	X	X					X		X
VR/#D Modeling					X			X				

Presentation Methods

Instructional Methods

Presentation Methods	Lecture	Role Play	Reading	Games	Demonstration	Simulation	Group Discussion	Practice	Case Study	Expert Panel	Programmed Instruction
Audio	X				X					X	
CBT			X					X			X
Electronic Text			X				X	X			X
EPSS			X		X	X	X	X	X		
Groupware			X				X	X	X		
Interactive TV	X			X	X		X	X	X	X	
Multimedia	X	X	X	X	X	X		X			X
Online Help			X								
Teleconferencing	X	X		X	X		X	X	X	X	
Video	X				X					X	
VR/#D Modeling				X	X	X					